In Search of God
in the
Sexual Underworld

In Search of God in the Sexual Underworld

A MYSTICAL JOURNEY

Edwin Clark Johnson

QUILL
New York   1983

The names or identifying characteristics of figures in this book have been changed whenever appropriate to maintain confidentiality. It is to the credit of most of those people I mention that they felt no need to hide their identities.

The author wishes to thank the following for permission to reprint copyrighted material:

Joseph Campbell, *The Hero With a Thousand Faces*, Bollingen Series XVII. Copyright 1949 by Princeton University Press. Copyright © renewed 1976 by Princeton University Press. Excerpt reprinted by permission of Princeton University Press.

Leonard Cohen, "The Lyric," copyright © 1966 by Project Seven Music, a division of Continental Total Media Project, Inc., 515 Madison Avenue, New York, N.Y. 10022.

Frederick Franck, from *The Book of Angelus Silesius,* by Frederick Franck. Copyright © 1976 by Frederick Franck. Reprinted by permission of Alfred A. Knopf, Inc.

Library of Congress Cataloging in Publication Data

Johnson, Edwin Clark.
  In search of God in the sexual underworld.

   1. Sex—Religious aspects. 2. Sex—Moral and ethical aspects. 3. Prostitution, Juvenile—United States.
I. Title.
HQ23.J63 1983b   306.7   83-2883
ISBN 0-688-01478-X
ISBN 0-688-02046-1 (pbk.)

Printed in the United States of America

First Quill Edition

1 2 3 4 5 6 7 8 9 10

BOOK DESIGN BY PATTY LOWY

For Mama
    who manifested in me
God's creative will

For Cam
    who manifested God's beauty and
love for creation

In honor of Avalokitesvara
    who reveals these two are one

Contents

And for all this, nature is never spent;
  There lives the dearest freshness deep down things;
And though the last lights off the black West went
  Oh, morning, at the brown brink eastward, springs—
Because the Holy Ghost over the bent
  World broods with warm breast and with ah! bright wings.

G. M. HOPKINS

INTRODUCTION

God and Sex

"God and sex," Robin remarked. "Is there anything else worth talking about?"

"Well," I replied, "people sure talk about sex all the time, but I don't know about God—at least not in the same breath. I'm a religion scholar. I talk about God a lot. And I talk about sex. But certainly the last thing in the world I expected was to become an expert on prostitution."

I was chatting away an autumn afternoon in San Francisco with Leslie, one of my housemates, and Robin, her friend from school days. I had been describing the research I was doing on one of the most disturbing dimensions of modern sexuality. During the past year I'd worked in a federally funded study of juvenile prostitution and "sexploitation." In order to understand life in this sexual underworld, I'd lived for a while in San Francisco's Tenderloin District and in New York's Times Square.

"I think you're right that spirituality and sexuality are the two major concerns of human life," I continued. "I'm not sure how they're reconciled, though I think they need to be. The prostitution project raised some very difficult questions for me."

An interest in God has traditionally been presumed to require transcending the world of money, power, and sex. In that spirit, as a young man I had "fled the world" in the age-old tradition of Christian monasticism and entered Roman Catholic religious life in order to pursue my interest in God. But the more I was exposed to religious thought, the more I found that the traditional religious assumptions were being undercut by contemporary events. One of those assumptions was that sex could be transcended. Psychology was showing that sexual concerns pervade all of life and that good mental health requires dealing consciously with sexual feelings. Sex was being looked at in a new way.

Indeed, during the seven years I was involved with monasticism and for about the same number of years afterward, while I was studying comparative religion and Jungian psychology, there was a "sexual revolution" in America. This revolution had been a long time in the making. It came about partly because of the insights of Sigmund Freud and others and the subsequent spread of psychological sophistication in modern society, and partly because of the development of effective and available contraceptives. It stemmed from demographic changes, resulting especially from the "baby boom" and rapid urbanization. It was incubated by the peace and prosperity of the 1950s, hastened by the rebellion against convention and conformity of the '60s, and colored by the cynicism and economic downturn of the '70s. It was fomented, as Gay Talese has observed, both by a few visible proponents, like Hugh Hefner, who had access to media and high technology and by activists in grassroots movements for sexual equality and liberation.

At root what wrought this revolution was simply the advance of knowledge. Information about genetics, endocrinology, epidemiology and psychology has cut through superstitious notions about sex from which traditional attitudes had been derived. Facts are now known. Old issues have been resolved. New issues have arisen.

The advance of knowledge has played havoc with religion in many arenas, but perhaps in none so much as those involving sexual behavior. In the context of contemporary socio-sexual realities, there seems little place for God. For many, religion no longer provides the sense of meaning it once did. Next to the new morality of sexually active moderns, traditional moral views and values seem life-denying and benighted. The beliefs of most religions seem doctrinaire, psychologically naive, and obsolete.

During my years of religious study I struggled to understand the nature of religion in the light of modern realities. In my first book, *The Myth of the Great Secret: A Search for Spiritual Meaning in the Face of Emptiness,* I described my discovery that in the pluralistic world brought about by international travel and communication the notion of a single religious "Truth" makes no sense. There are too many different religious truths. The function of religion today should not be to promulgate correct doctrine, but to provide patterns by which people can give meaning to their lives. God is found and worshipped, I believe, in the perception of meaning in our everyday experience. We "invent" meaning in our lives by associating our personal experiences with the deeply rooted symbols that have been the significant content of religion and myth through the ages.

Thus to find God, and so to make my own life worthwhile, I looked at how I interpreted coincidences and imposed subjective meaning on events. Using the symbols and archetypes of myth and religion I had learned so much about in religious life, I wove a pattern of meaning into my experience. I saw life as a complex Rorschach test. I was amazed to find how clearly messages presented themselves and how easily I could follow the clues.

In the fall of 1977 the clues led me to work with Toby Marotta, a Harvard-trained social scientist interested in liberationist politics and socio-sexual change. After producing three books together, in 1979 we began working on a study of juvenile prostitution with Urban and Rural Systems Associates, a private consulting firm based in San Francisco. The study exposed me to sexuality in ways I'd never imagined, and my religious beliefs challenged me to make sense of that experience.

In the course of the study, I saw squalor and suffering. I saw wasted lives. I saw sex at its most blatant and commercial. I saw an underworld that most people never see. And I also saw that none of these things were what most people think they are. Popular conceptions of prostitution and pornography are simply inaccurate. And the suffering in the sexual underworld is, at least partly, the result of these misconceptions. I saw that God is active in the sexual underworld, albeit in perplexing ways. In fact, at least among some residents of the Tenderloin, God is just as much a concern as it is for me.

Robin was fascinated with my observations. Not unlike many of our generation, she thought that sex was good for people. She enjoyed falling in love and acknowledged frankly that the idea of settling down with a single partner for the rest of her life and having children didn't appeal to her. And she was just as interested in the issues of religion and morality. She practiced daily meditation, read the writings of mystics and spiritual teachers of different religious traditions, and attended several churches and ashrams.

Now twenty-eight, she'd grown up during the 1960s. Her experience of sex, love, and relationship had been shaped less by conventional attitudes than by the counterculture, hippie consciousness, and the sexual revolution. Early in her life she'd seen that sex could be fun, liberating, and, once she'd learned to overcome possessiveness and dependency, a source of emotional richness and growth for herself and her partners. Her own experiences had led her to question the taboos of traditional religion. Indeed, she'd come to believe that the mainstream Churches were more concerned with maintaining middle-class arrangements and values than with inspiring the spiritual vision she was seeking. The Oriental and esoteric religions appealed to her because they promoted practices that induced such vision.

Robin was a good person. She was remarkably kind, delightfully vivacious, loving, generous, and responsible. If "sexual promiscuity" made people vicious, selfish, debauched, and irreligious, one would never know it from looking at her. Indeed, she believed her sexual experience had made her more virtuous and religious. She also believed that her religiousness, by creating a context of meaning, had in turn enhanced her experience of sex and protected her from becoming neurotic, self-centered, debauched, or degraded. Sex and God—to Robin the two didn't seem antagonistic at all, and should not be made to seem so.

Her perspective was not unfamiliar to me. When I had left religious life in 1970, feeling that the Church wasn't dealing with modern reality, I'd turned to the counterculture and the Movement. There I'd found a moral sensibility that urged peace and love and championed a vision of men and women living in harmony with themselves and the world. Far more than the mainstream religions, the countercultural vision seemed to offer an ethics for modern life.

For most people, however, and even in what Robin and I would consider our own generation, sex and God have been thought to be antagonistic. God, through the religions, has seemed more concerned with repressing sexual instincts than with encouraging positive and ethical attitudes toward life. The religions have seemed more obsessed with governing sexual relationships than with instructing followers in practices to expand consciousness beyond ego, or with encouraging virtue in dealing with major social issues like affluence, energy consumption, ecological pollution, consumer fraud, tax evasion, oppression of minorities, or war.

The Churches' failure to be realistic in the face of the vast socio-sexual and cultural changes that mark modern life has deterred many from discovering spirituality. This failure has also left few moral guidelines for those who have rejected obsolete religious rules. Some, like Robin, have been successful in constructing value systems that help them lead happy and fulfilled lives. But many others have not been successful. They have become lonely and jaded. They have come to manifest the worst qualities of what has been called the culture of narcissism. They

have become self-centered, materialistic in the extreme, and cynical about love. In their effort to vindicate their enjoyment of
sexual pleasure, they have stripped their reality of everything but
pleasure, leaving it flat and meaningless

It has been said—I believed this myself for a time—that the
modern age has lost its moral fiber, that vice and sin are winning
over the masses because people can't resist temptation. But that
"temptation" is simply to live according to modern, scientifically
based standards. And the fact is that these standards are inevita-
bly going to supplant traditional religious ones, if only because,
as religion scholar Jacob Needleman observes in *A Sense of the
Cosmos,* science creates a "wall of certainty" that naive faith
simply cannot knock down. Nor should it try to. The biggest
challenge facing the spiritually-minded today is to discover the
meaning of God *in the terms of the modern world.* Like many
Jungian and Transpersonal psychologists and scholars of mythology, I believe that this can be accomplished by using the
age-old patterns in the religious and mythical traditions to interpret contemporary experience.

In *The Hero with a Thousand Faces,* Joseph Campbell, one of
the foremost scholars of mythology, describes the central theme
of all myth as the hero's journey. The mythical hero is led out
of the secure world of everyday reality to venture into an underworld where he must battle with demons in order finally to see
God and to discover his own deepest identity. The hero can then
return to the world bearing boons, for he has learned the secret
of transformation. He knows who he really is. The hero portrayed in myth and legend is the symbol of the self in each of us.
We are all called to seek our deepest identity.

This book is the story of how I pursued such a journey, leaving
my secure world and entering an underworld, in order to seek
the truth of my own life and a truth for modern times. It is an
account of how I wrestled with questions that must be of as much
concern to advocates of a new morality as they are to proponents

of traditional moralities. This book is a report on the juvenile prostitution study—not, of course, the report the government paid for, which URSA has delivered to its federal employers—but the one my heart compelled me to write in order to understand my world in terms of mythic symbols. Hence the book is both the tapestry of meaning I have woven out of my experience and the boon I brought back with me. I hope that the insights into the nature of spirit, consciousness, and virtue I have gained will be useful to other seekers who are struggling to find guidelines for behavior in the midst of the dazzling world of modern sexuality.

In a sense, then, this book is a companion to Toby Marotta's *Hustlers, Hookers, Johns and Janes.* His book is an elaboration of the ethnographic and sociological work on male prostitution and sexual social change he undertook for URSA. Mine is a description of the philosophical insights we shared. To the government, through URSA, we submitted findings and recommendations. To the readers of these books we submit the "truths" behind those findings and recommendations.

Some readers may be put off by my tendency to be soft on "sinners" and hard on religion. It is likely that more religious people than sinners are going to pick up a book with the word "God" on the cover. While "sexual underworld" may attract a few others, my guess is that for most who read this book the spiritual life is already an interest. It is you whom I want to shock into seeing the world in a different way.

For millennia, religious people have been condemning sinners. These condemnations have had little effect on the amount of sin in the world. They have, however, excluded many from hearing the "good news" of spiritual reality and diminished the degree to which others have enjoyed life. In the name of such condemnations governments have, in the past, executed sinners, and more recently, established penal and social service systems to rehabilitate them. Yet one of the things I saw most clearly in my research of programs for juvenile prostitutes is that such interventions tend as often to perpetuate the problems as to solve them.

Jesus Christ changed the world, not nearly as much through the institution that followed him as through the message he taught. After all, it is not institutions that shape history but attitudes; not changes in regimes and systems but changes in consciousness. We who think of ourselves as spiritual can really only change the world by changing ourselves. And almost all the spiritual teachers have said that the proper direction of that change is toward understanding and forgiving.

Jesus condemned very few people. He never condemned the sinners. But he did condemn the leaders of the institutional Church of his day.

PART I

With Ah!
Bright Wings

Angel of God, my guardian dear,
to whom God's love entrusts me here,
ever this day, be at my side to lead and guard,
to rule and guide. Amen.

THE BALTIMORE CATECHISM

ONE

Following the Path of Adventure

The hero's journey begins with "the call to adventure." A mysterious event causes the prospective hero to break with the life he has been leading and to search after some treasure or some secret knowledge, useful for himself or for his family or tribe. In the search, he encounters obstacles and endures trials by which he proves himself worthy. Sometimes he meets a mate. He is often guided by omens or by a messenger. The messenger points out the way and teaches him how to overcome the obstacles and find what he is seeking.

The Biblical Tobias, for instance, was sent by his blind father on a journey into a strange land to seek repayment of a debt which would help the old man in his tribulation. Tobias was guided by an angel who came to him in the guise of a beautiful young man. On the first night of their journey, Tobias was attacked by a monstrous fish when he went to the river to wash. The angel taught him that the entrails of the monster possessed magical powers. The liver protected Tobias from a devil that had slain seven husbands of the woman to whom he was betrothed. And when he returned from his journey, as the angel instructed him, the gall restored his father's sight.

Not unlike Tobias, the diminutive of whose name I've gone by all my life, I was guided by an angel on my journey into the sexual underworld. Like Tobias, I was taught by my angel how, with the magic of the monsters that lurk in that world, vision can be transformed.

* * *

The day my angel first appeared I was doing intake at the community mental health clinic in San Francisco's Tenderloin District where I worked. It was my job that afternoon to see whoever came into the clinic to determine how we could help them. I'd dealt with several cases. One of them had been difficult; I was tired and annoyed with the whole mental health system. I'd thought I was through for the day. I was disappointed to find another chart stuck in the intake rack.

I looked around the waiting room. Sitting on the far side was a rather shabbily dressed old woman I recognized as a clinic regular. One of the large population of "burnt-out" schizophrenics who've ended up in the Tenderloin, she was one of many whom the clinic supplied with occasional "TLC" and regular maintenance doses of anti-psychotic medication. Sitting near the door was a good-looking man making notes on a clipboard resting in his lap as he paged through a sheaf of papers. He looked in his early thirties—about my own age, I guessed. He was dressed in blue jeans and blue chambray work shirt, not very different from my own choice of clothes that day. His wire-frame glasses, with a sheathing of tortoiseshell rimming circular lenses, gave him an owlish look. The green canvas book bag on the floor between his feet added to the academic appearance.

I pulled what I assumed to be his chart from the rack. Inside the folder, instead of the usual pink intake questionnaire prospective clients were asked to fill out, was a note from the receptionist:

> Toby,
>   Would you please talk to this man.
>   His name is Toby Marotta.

Apparently he wasn't a client. I looked at his first name a second time to be sure I'd read it correctly.

"Mr. Marotta," I called.

He looked up, smiled warmly, tucked the papers he'd been studying onto the clipboard, and stood up. Throwing the book bag over his shoulder, he stepped toward me and extended his hand.

As we shook hands, I introduced myself, initiating an exchange that we would jokingly and affectionately continue for years to come.

"Hi, I'm Toby."

"Hi, I'm Toby."

We laughed as I showed him into an interview room. "What can I do for you?"

Toby explained that he was working for Central City Hospitality House, the neighborhood community center just around the corner from the clinic. He and several co-workers were studying the Tenderloin. They wanted to learn its history, understand its character, and assess its social service needs. Toby was currently interviewing service providers in the various social service agencies located in the neighborhood. He said he was especially interested in the Tenderloin Clinic because it had a reputation for being avant-garde and progressive.

In response, I explained how the clinic operated, stressing that we had developed a social and political perspective on what was wrong with our clients and were determined to do more for them than simply maintain them on drugs. The clinic had also developed a special outreach to the large population of homosexual men and women in the neighborhood and the city, I explained. Toby was especially interested in this and pressed me further.

Though it appeared to be only a sleazy heterosexual "red light district," the Tenderloin was the home of a good many homosexuals. Some of these people had emotional problems and needed help, I added. Some had previously gone to psychiatrists who, for reasons known only to the doctors, were more interested in "treating" their sexuality than in helping them with their problems. Because of such stories of mistreatment, many gay people in San Francisco who could benefit from crisis intervention counseling or from therapy for psychosomatic complaints were reluctant to go to any sort of mental health clinic.

To reach these people, the San Francisco Department of Health financed the Tenderloin Clinic as one of the first so-called "gay-supportive" counseling programs in the country. A number of the professionals on the staff were well-adjusted, out-front gay men or lesbians. All on the staff were committed to providing mental health care that wasn't simply conventional socialization or an extension of police power over the minds of those who, for whatever reason, found themselves deviant in mainstream American society.

I explained my own history with the clinic. I'd been an intern there while in a postgraduate program in counseling psychology and after getting my degree I'd taken the first job that had become available because I'd liked working there. It was certainly very different from the traditional psychiatric hospitals in which I'd been employed.

We'd talked way beyond the thirty or forty minutes usually set aside for an intake. Toby had a clipboard full of notes about the clinic, its history, its two different clienteles (the neighborhood psychiatric patients and the gay men and lesbians), and the problems involved in serving both of them out of the same agency. But I still didn't know much about his Tenderloin study. I was interested in hearing more of that. And I was curious about his own history, and especially how he'd come by the name Toby.

He pointed to his green book bag. He was from Cambridge, a Harvard student, still enrolled in a Ph.D. program there. He'd recently moved to Berkeley with his lover of some ten years to complete his dissertation on the politics of homosexuality. He'd been hired by Hospitality House to study life in the Tenderloin. He was particularly interested in the job because he had heard the district was an old gay neighborhood and his long-term plan was to study the origins and evolution of gay life in San Francisco.

He intended to begin by exploring the gay male subculture in the Tenderloin as an anthropologist would explore a foreign tribe. This, he stressed, was an important issue of methodology. Most studies of "deviant" populations were done by detached social scientists who sat in comfortable offices and designed questionnaires to be administered to counselors or clients of social service agencies or people involved in the criminal justice system. That would certainly give a picture of troubled and troublesome elements in the inner city, he argued, but it wouldn't describe what the people's lives were really like and how they actually felt about themselves, and it certainly didn't demonstrate respect for their choice of life-styles. Toby's ethnographic approach was to be very different.

For starters, he'd moved into a hotel in the heart of the lower Tenderloin so that he could gain the trust of the residents and experience life as they did. Such an approach, he believed, was the only way really to understand and to assess unconventional subcultures, and it was also the only way to study those who were part of them without further impairing their self-worth.

If I'd known then what my own involvement in ethnography was going to cost me financially and psychologically, I might have shied away from Toby completely. As it was, I responded positively to his ideas about research methodology and to his liberationist views about respecting individual difference and social diversity. By the time I met Toby, I had been convinced by my exploration of religion and metaphysics that value is a subjective creation of the mind, judgments and opinions only keep us imprisoned: life here and now deserves to be affirmed regardless of what it looks like.

So I agreed with his ideas, but realized that their application to Tenderloin types was going to be a real challenge. In truth, like most people my impulse was to believe that there were certain types of behavior that should not be and certain forms of social interaction that should be eradicated from society. I had seen suffering and wasted human potential in the mental patients I'd worked with over the years. I had walked through the Tenderloin with strong feelings that something had to be done about the neighborhood, that some of its inhabitants should be removed, that their lives and habitats were eyesores, and that their querulousness, alcoholism, drug abuse, and amorality were unconscionable. Indeed, as a religiously inspired person, I had devoted myself to doing something to alleviate what I perceived as their unmitigated suffering. But I wasn't about to live among them.

Toby's ideas challenged me to apply my philosophical abstractions to reality. "Oh, I certainly don't mean that people *should* live like this," he hastened to add, "or that nothing should be done to improve their conditions. The point of the study is to make recommendations that might better life in the neighborhood. But I do mean that to find out what life here is really all about and to make realistic suggestions, we must get the truth from the residents' perspective. And we can do this only if we approach them and their situations with respect."

I admired Toby's idealism, his obvious intelligence and articulateness, and his curious innocence in being so moral in approaching people and activities that so many in society—especially in the name of religion—considered immoral.

When the receptionist peered through the window into the interview room I noticed the hour. The clinic was closing. It was time for both of us to go home.

"But I never got to ask about your name," I complained.

"Then we'll have to get together again soon," he rejoined.

I invited him to sit in on the rap group David Greenberg and I ran for neighborhood residents. He accepted. He said he'd like to see more of the clinic.

Another man named Toby! A curious coincidence, I thought as I showed him out the door and got ready to go home. We'd obviously liked each other and one another's ideas. Would the coincidence of name be a sign of some deeper connection?

*   *   *

The next week Toby attended the meeting of the drop-in group. Afterward we went to one of the seedier bars in the Tenderloin for a beer and some immersion in the life of the neighborhood. Toby was doing ethnographic research. I was pursuing my fascination with this man who called himself by my name and who, I was discovering, espoused many of the same beliefs and values I did.

There were many similarities in our lives. We'd both been given Toby as a childhood nickname. Except in passing, neither of us had known other Tobys. We both had parents who by dint of hard work, good fortune, and concern for their families had managed to provide their children with opportunities for education and social advancement they themselves had lacked. Our fathers had both died during our freshman years of high school, leaving us to grow into adulthood perhaps a little sooner than we otherwise would have. We had both been leaders in our classes, teachers' pets, whiz kids of one sort or another.

Born in Boston, Toby had found it natural to look to Harvard as a choice for college. Growing up in San Antonio in the Texas heartland I really had not known where Harvard was. But I'd been fascinated with science as a boy and aspired to a career as an astrophysicist. I told everyone I was going to go to M.I.T. I had, in fact, initiated the process that would have brought me to Cambridge and perhaps to a meeting with Toby Marotta in 1963 instead of 1977, but I dropped the application upon deciding to enter religious life after high school.

Toby had gone on to graduate school at Harvard, developed expertise in the study of social science and social policy, and— with that zeal to integrate the personal, political, and professional and to change the world that was so characteristic of our sixties generation—turned his attention to the study of gay life. I'd "fled the world" but had felt that same zeal. For me, being spiritually conscious was the way to integrate my life and to improve the world.

Now, fifteen years later, we were carrying similar values and commitments into practice by trying to understand and to change the way society, often unwittingly and unwillingly though no less viciously, imposed suffering on so many of those who did not conform to traditional standards and conventional expectations.

Our lives complemented one another. We were born in the same year, 1945, almost exactly six months apart. Toby had been born at the end of January under the sign of Aquarius; I'd been born at the beginning of August under the sign of Leo. Neither of us, of course, was so naive as to take astrology literally, but we were conscious enough of symbology and mythology to appreciate the significance we could impute to that coincidence: Our horoscopes were in some respects mirror images of one another.

Our generation had championed the notion of "revolution through consciousness change." We believed that we could live good lives by "actualizing ourselves," heeding our own hearts, and exploring and experiencing whatever we wanted so long as that didn't hurt anyone else and promised to "raise consciousness." We were deeply affected by the hopeless and meaningless war in Southeast Asia. We came to believe that the most effective strategy for bringing peace and transforming society was changing the way people thought about themselves, and everybody else. To do this, we had to withdraw from the "system" and develop new ways of thinking and living that would make our lives examples others would want to follow. The result, we argued, would be a snowballing of individual changes of consciousness that would renew American society.

At the time Toby and I met, I still thought of myself as a radical, but I'd come to see that for the revolution we envisioned it was not necessary that capitalism be overthrown, the military-industrial complex dismantled, or the laws against marijuana repealed. I'd realized that the truly radical act was to live as virtuously as possible, to tell the truth always, and to strive to be compassionate and understanding. That was the vision of a good society that had led our generation to declare itself a counterculture in the first place.

But by 1977, the summer of love had been over for a decade. The term counterculture was generally ridiculed. The Age of Aquarius appeared to have been aborted. The revolution seemed to have come and gone without producing the expected results. Like so many who'd been idealistic and enthusiastic in the '60s, I felt disillusioned and defeated.

That season the rock group Kansas had a popular song called "Dust in the Wind." It reminded me of our expectations—that I was mortal and that all I accomplished was going to die with me. On the one hand, it was consoling to realize that nothing ultimately mattered. But it grieved me as well. I wanted my life to be worthwhile, so that the world would be better because I'd been here. I still believed it was possible to change the world by example, but I wasn't sure I was doing it anymore. I didn't know if working in mental health really did good. I sometimes seemed to be nothing more than a modern-day Inquisitor. I didn't know if the values I believed in had produced an attractive and imitable personality or if they had resulted only in self-obsession. And by this time, the counterculture was being derided as a culture of narcissism.

To me the countercultural values of love for one another, freedom to be oneself, support of individual and social difference, and avoidance of phoniness and conformity to norms antithetical to self-actualization had been modern-day manifestations of the Christian virtues of love, truthfulness, respect for others, and rejection of legalism and hypocrisy. I saw that the counterculture had called people to be open and kind, caring for others and comfortable with themselves, properly indignant at the sight of injustice, but not pushy or demanding and, most of all, vital, interesting, and interested—attentive to others' lives because only there could be found the substance of truth.

In Toby Marotta I saw manifested these countercultural values. Of course, sometimes Toby seemed oblivious to things I thought important, overbearing, self-obsessed, cocky, and superior. He struck me as being too easily impressed by the opinions of the Eastern Establishment and slightly scornful of those who did not share his taste in opinion-makers. At times he even seemed petty and possessive. But these traits could hardly be called vices; they were simply personality characteristics. Overriding them I found a zest for life, a marvelous assumption of other people's good intentions, and a faith that even in the face of adversity things were going to work out. These were the virtues by which I, too, strove to live. That I was to some extent projecting my own values onto Toby, perhaps because I was infatuated with him and his Bostonian mystique, does not lessen the positive influence he had on me. By coming to know him, I came also to know myself better. All that sorrow about being mere dust in the wind faded. My work got better, and I think my clients did, too.

Toby was a kind of mirror for me, a manifestation by the universe of myself in the form of another—another with almost my own past and with my own name. In him I could see how my beliefs and values affected a life. I liked the example I saw. Toby became a confirmation of my efforts to live as I believed all should. As the weeks passed and we came to know one another better, often over mugs of beer after the drop-in group, I began to imagine Toby Marotta as a messenger from God, come to reassure me and lead me on my journey. Indeed, I saw him as an incarnation of my Guardian Angel.

In the Servite Order, which I'd joined toward the end of college, I'd taken Peregrine as a ritual name. It means wanderer. It had been the name of a Servite saint. A curious part of his legend, a part I did not learn until sometime after I'd begun to mythologize Toby as my Guardian Angel, is that Saint Peregrine had also been given an angel for a companion. Though I left the Servites after three years, I kept my identity as Peregrine the

wanderer, including, apparently, the angel guide. One evening
the angel made me a proposition that called me, in Campbell's
terms, to "cross the first threshold."

Toby completed his dissertation on gay political activity a few
months after we met. I'd completed my own dissertation shortly
before. Mine, a world away from his, was on the nature of
mythology and the problem of finding meaning in the modern,
technological world.

Both of us wanted to publish our work. But dissertations by
their very nature require extensive revision to make them into
readable, marketable books. Faced with that chore, I'd left mine
sitting on the back corner of my desk, telling myself I'd get to
it one day. Toby was more committed to getting his published
right away, but no less appalled by the job.

"Writing is such a lonely task," he observed one evening after
dinner at my house. "It would be so much easier if I had some
help."

"I'll help you," I offered impulsively.

"And I could help you with yours."

The idea of doing the work together made it seem possible.
There and then we made a pact to help one another revise our
dissertations and get them published. We agreed to divide the
costs and possible rewards, to help each other explain shared
ideals from complimentary perspectives, to keep each other true
to those ideals, and maybe to get ourselves famous.

Toby was insistent about becoming prominent. At Harvard
he'd been trained to value public recognition as evidence of
achievement. In the monastery, I'd been taught to value humility
and self-abnegation. My goal in life was to be good, to please
God, to be a hero. I was in search of a truth more profound than
book reviews or limelight.

"I'm not talking about limelight," he responded when I objected to his ideas about recognition. "I agree that humility is a
virtue." He had few illusions about the value of fame over the

long run. But in the short run, he said, it was necessary to touch individual lives if one was to better society. To do that the books had to be reviewed and read. The theory of revolution through consciousness change, he maintained, suggested that the way to change culture was to infiltrate it, to transform the system by succeeding in its terms, then to use that success to establish new values. "You're not much of a hero," he said, "if you just sit on your knowledge and enjoy your wisdom and share it with no one."

According to Campbell's analysis, the last step of the hero's journey is to bring boons back into the world. Suddenly Toby seemed less like my friend the Harvard graduate talking about fame and fortune and more like the Angel with bright wings pointing out an obligation on my spiritual path.

For the next several months we worked, separately and together, to revise Toby's manuscript into the book that Houghton Mifflin published in the spring of 1981 as *The Politics of Homosexuality.* Then through mutual agreement we began to work on *Sons of Harvard,* a book that our agent, John Brockman, thought would make us some money and get some recognition. Toby saw *Sons of Harvard,* a series of interviews with classmates of his, as a vehicle for popularizing the themes of his scholarship. He wanted to use these lives to illustrate the idea of liberation through consciousness change. We completed *Sons of Harvard* —with much less smoothness and ease than this capsule chronology suggests—and started on the revision of my dissertation that would be published by William Morrow in greatly changed form as *The Myth of the Great Secret.*

Very different from Toby's, my book also explained how the countercultural worldviews that became popular during the '60s had influenced American society. Each of us in our own ways believed the new morality of our generation was the best hope for a more humane future. Both of us felt that the problems of the new morality could be better solved by pursuing the ideals of that morality responsibly than by reverting back to an old morality or by giving up and becoming cynical and materialistic.

We recognized that the process of liberation we championed involved new social problems. Changes in sexual morality were altering traditional ideas about relationships. Models of successful relationships in the context of sexual liberation were rare. Teenagers were becoming sexually active much younger. Working in the Tenderloin, for instance, both of us had noticed the teenagers, especially males, engaging in sexual activity that had traditionally been called prostitution. If they were to have any lasting value, we believed, our countercultural outlooks and liberationist politics had to have something sensible to say about such contemporary sexual and social problems as juvenile prostitution.

While in Washington, D.C., to interview one of his classmates for *Sons of Harvard,* Toby learned of an upcoming federal project to study juvenile prostitution. He returned enthusiastic about the possibility of our being hired by a San Francisco consulting firm to work on it. I shared his enthusiasm and so soon, following my Guardian Angel, I found myself on the road right into the heart of the sexual underworld.

Juvenile prostitution was being perceived as a growing problem in modern America. Documentaries were appearing on television, articles in newspapers and magazines. An increasing number of troubled teenagers who came to youth agencies were reporting experience in prostitution. The agencies were having difficulty working with these sexually active kids, and they guessed that many others, recognizing this, were not coming for help at all.

Officials in the Youth Development Bureau in the Department of Health and Human Services, which coordinated the network of runaway and youth programs, believed it important to understand this phenomenon. In the fall of 1980, they issued a Request For Proposals to study it to consulting and research firms across the country.

Because a significant amount of research had been or was being done on prostitution by females, including juveniles, but little had been done on prostitution by males, especially involving juveniles, the RFP asked for a review of existing literature on female prostitution and for original research on male prostitution. These findings, from fieldwork and from visits to agencies with programs directed to juvenile prostitutes, plus appropriate recommendations were to be incorporated into a resource manual for social policymakers and service providers.

Toby had learned that Urban and Rural Systems Associates, a private consulting firm in San Francisco respected for its research, training, and program evaluations involving children, adolescents, and families in crisis could bid for the YDB contract. We contacted URSA and offered to do the required field research.

URSA's offices were in a renovated warehouse among the ruins of San Francisco's once prosperous Port Authority. A block from the Ferry Building, with east windows opening onto the Bay, URSA claimed the paradoxically modest, but classy address Pier 1½. The offices were unassuming but attractive.

Toby and I were impressed with the open-mindedness we found in the men and women working there. Most of them were veterans of the Movement of the '60s, liberals, counterculturalists, and liberationists who'd found in the consulting business a way to use expertise they'd developed through their earlier participation in politics and community organizing. Some had been service providers in grassroots agencies. Several were now Ph.D.'s, others lawyers. Almost all of them believed that public interest research was a vehicle for social progress.

URSA seemed impressed with us. They liked our realistic attitudes and our ideas about research. Toby talked knowledgeably about male prostitution and gay life on the basis of the ethnographic work he'd done for Hospitality House. I spoke of my experiences with Tenderloin residents at the clinic. Both of us seemed hard-headed, no-nonsense types who hadn't fallen for moralistic rhetoric. We had entree into the demimonde to be studied through people we knew from our political, mental health, and social service backgrounds. And we were willing to risk danger and endure discomfort in order to bring URSA a firsthand report.

After URSA agreed to bid for the contract to study juvenile prostitution, we sat down with staff to explain what we knew about the phenomenon and how we thought it could most effectively be researched. We recommended an ethnographic approach. We agreed to move into the Tenderloin in San Francisco and Times Square in New York so that we could see firsthand how hustling fit into life in these locales and interview participants in contexts in which they would feel natural and comfortable. We planned also to interview personnel in a variety of traditional and non-traditional social service programs: runaway shelters, prostitute self-help groups, gay community service centers, police and welfare departments.

Over a couple of weeks we developed a research proposal. URSA presented this as its bid to undertake work for the federal government. We won the contract.

In addition to URSA's regular consultant staff, three people were hired to work on the study. At the beginning, each of us assumed duties we were best suited to by our previous experience. Toby Marotta, as an experienced researcher on the homosexual male subculture, took responsibility for the field research on adolescent male prostitution. Kelly Weisberg, as a sociologist turned lawyer who'd worked with URSA previously on a study of family violence, took responsibility for the review of literature on juvenile female prostitution. And I, as a mental health worker who'd had experience in social service planning, took responsibility for the reports on existing agencies. URSA partners Noel Day, Bruce Fisher, and Ernie Fazio shared various responsibilities for directing the study and coordinating with Darryl Summers, our government project officer. To Michele Magee, Noel Day's competent and resourceful young assistant, fell the responsibility for organizing everyone and keeping us on schedule.

We spent a couple of months reviewing literature, telephoning agencies across the country, and planning for the fieldwork and site visits. Toby and I began spending more and more time hanging out in the Tenderloin, then pretty soon rented rooms for ourselves in two adjoining hotels in the center of that sex-trade zone.

TWO

Descent
into the Underworld

Along the journey the mythic hero sometimes meets the Wise
Old Man. This may be a threshold guardian, a taskmaster, or
judge who imposes some ordeal. He may be a teacher or spiritual
Master. In any case, the Wise Old Man possesses knowledge the
hero needs, and to learn it the hero must often give up something
of himself.

The study of prostitution was, of course, not going to be the first
experience of the Tenderloin for either Toby Marotta or me.
Toby had spent a year directing the Tenderloin Ethnographic
Research Project. His work had immersed him deeply in the life
of the neighborhood. I had worked for two years at the Tenderloin Clinic. But I'd been protected by my role as a mental health
worker. When I first began working at the clinic, I'd avoided the
heart of the Tenderloin, a few blocks downtown from our offices.
I hadn't thought there could be anything in the neighborhood for
me, other than the opportunity to perform the service for suffering souls I felt my spiritual life demanded. I certainly hadn't
thought I'd find any interest in spiritual matters among the
denizens.

My assumptions about Tenderloin residents were challenged
when I took on Harry Edwards as a client. His life, as different
from mine as day from night but in some ways just as spiritually
motivated, forced me to rethink my ideas about the Tenderloin.
He became my Wise Old Man. And through me he became a
guide to the neighborhood for Toby Marotta as well.

Harry was in his mid-fifties. He came into the clinic seeking help after spending a night with his feet dangling over the edge of the roof of the dilapidated apartment building in which he lived. He said he didn't see any reason to go on. He'd wasted his life; he'd failed to accomplish anything worthwhile; and now even his spiritual life had withered away. Especially because he'd mentioned the spiritual life, I kept Harry as my own client.

Harry had grown up in Detroit, the son of a devout Christian Science mother who'd taught him that the world was illusion and that love and positive thinking could overcome sickness and evil. Though no longer an active Christian Scientist, he still believed that and tried to act on it. After a variety of jobs that included selling everything from buttons to automobiles, Harry found his real talent in writing song lyrics to popular tunes. It was the mid '50s and rock 'n' roll was changing the music industry. Dick Clark's *American Bandstand* was one of the country's most popular TV shows. Harry found himself a sales job in the booming record business. He was hired because he could write lyrics and knew musicians and because he was affable and bold.

Because the success of a particular record depended on its being played on the radio, a major part of selling records was getting air time. Harry was one of the men who entertained DJs, did them favors, and sometimes tipped them for playing a particular record.

Rock 'n' roll signaled the beginning of what would later be called the generation gap. Parents didn't understand and didn't like the music their children were listening to. Elvis Presley did not seem a proper role model. He moved his hips too much and his name sounded like pelvis. He was too obviously sexual. In an effort to police the industry, the exchange of favors and tips between record company representatives and radio station personnel, dubbed payola by the media, was deemed unethical and illegal.

Harry was a victim of the payola scandal. Though for a moment in his life he achieved national recognition (his name appeared in *Time* magazine), his career was ruined. He was not sent to jail, but the whole affair broke his spirit. He ended up an outcast, living among the low-life in California. Soon he suffered a beating that left him disabled for a time and got him on Aid to the Totally Disabled (A.T.D.), which would later become S.S.I. (Supplemental Security Income)—the federal subsidy most people know as welfare. With the prospect of a guaranteed check from the government, he no longer tried to work.

He was still affable and bold, though, and soon became something of a local character. He befriended derelicts, runaway kids, and others down on their luck. He brought newcomers home and fed them for a while if they'd help around the house, chip in a little for the food, and maybe have sex with him. And he helped them get acclimated. Harry probably managed to save a few lives.

Barry, Harry's companion of fourteen years through much of the turmoil, had recently developed a brain tumor. And though the tumor had been successfully removed, the surgery had left his face partially paralyzed, his mind dazed, and his nervous system subject to seizures. The two of them were living in a one-room apartment with five or six dogs and however many stray humans Harry would bring home to join "the family." By the time he came to see me, Harry felt burnt out from too many people passing through his life, too many drugs, too little stability. Life had become intolerable.

In clinical jargon, Harry was suffering from a "transitional crisis of later life." He had, we discovered, reached the age at which, years before, he'd prophesied he'd die. He was bored and depressed and needed a reason not to die as expected. In our sessions we talked about his spirituality. Throughout his entire history, however sordid it sounded, Harry had remained conscious of a mystical reality that supported his life. He'd read esoteric and mystical literature, maintained a life of prayer, and through a kind of haphazard meditation sought contact with the life force that transcended his individuality.

The drug culture of the late '60s had supported these interests;

he'd found many hippies and acid heads who'd loved to talk about mysticism. But in the '70s he'd sensed a loss of interest in such subjects, especially in the Tenderloin. His ordinary life gave him little occasion to talk about these concerns.

In me, Harry found another seeker, educated, serious, and respectable, unlike the acid heads. My affirmation of his spiritual quest and my encouragement that he repudiate his prophecy of dying and change his life began to make things different. In a couple of weeks his despondency passed. He continued to drop in to see me but we became more spiritual friends than client and therapist. I looked forward to his visits, knowing they'd be an opportunity for me to put aside business for a while and talk about spiritual concerns. I was often as unable to talk about that part of my life with my psychiatric colleagues as Harry was with his drug heads and derelicts.

Knowing that Toby Marotta would enjoy meeting such a neighborhood character and wanting, in part, to share with Harry the magic I'd found in Toby, I introduced them. Toby interviewed Harry for his study and, recognizing his knowledge of Tenderloin life, hired him as a research assistant.

Harry proved very effective in his role as guide to the neighborhood. He was a good reporter on his own experience and he'd been around long enough to have seen historical change in the Tenderloin. But his employment was not without its problems. Harry hadn't held a steady job in over a decade. He made errors of judgment. He was not altogether able to understand the difference between his own values and needs and those of the agency. But the job had gradually got him off welfare and showed him it was possible to discipline himself to come to work on schedule, budget time, and follow instructions. He saw he could live differently and that he felt better when he wasn't obligated to remain somehow disabled to secure his livelihood. Through the assistance of a now successful businessman, whom, once years before when he was down on his luck, Harry had taken in and cared for briefly, he got a respectable job and a place to live outside the low-life culture.

Harry was perhaps unusually fortunate. Most of the recipients of S.S.I. who live in the inner cities never manage to break out of the demoralizing and destructive cycle. There are those, of course, who receive disability payments because they are severely injured, paraplegic, blind, mentally retarded or brain damaged. For them, S.S.I. is a godsend. But there are many others who receive government support because of a psychiatric or personality disorder. They are caught in a terrible trap: their security depends on their remaining crazy, maladapted, unhappy, and poorly socialized.

S.S.I. eligibility requires that recipients have a difficult time working and relating to other people. Most of them, at least in the cities, end up living alone in substandard, but costly hotels, buying their food from cafes or overpriced corner groceries, and eating processed junk foods and cheap carbohydrates that provide minimal nutrition. They see a psychiatrist a couple of times a month for maintenance doses of medications that erase memory, deaden ego, and sap motivation; the medications flatten facial expression, frequently induce a form of Parkinson's tremors, and sometimes, after prolonged use, irreversible involuntary spastic motions of the tongue and jaws. The drugs make people look crazy. Because community mental health performs a kind of police function, preventing the mentally ill from being nuisances or from becoming violent, and because so many of the mentally ill are living in environments that would drive anybody crazy, therapists are reluctant to try taking their clients off medication and thus risk recurrence of the psychiatric disorder.

One way out of this life would be to move away from the highly stressful neighborhoods that perpetuate it. But most of these people don't have the opportunity to move into the country, and nowhere else but in inner cities can one rent a room without making a deposit or paying first and last months' rent.

Just as many middle-American renters find they can never accumulate the money for a down payment on their own home, so welfare recipients can seldom accumulate enough money to improve their situations.

Banding together in small communities of three, four, or five people would allow some to make such moves, but most of the mentally ill recipients of S.S.I. are so alienated and caught up in idiosyncratic habits that they can't manage to live with other people. And besides, successful community building would be a sign of socialization skills and could render them ineligible for their payments.

Harry was lucky. He escaped from the trap: partly because his disability had always been something of a sham (he was a wheeler-dealer who manipulated the doctors into giving him medications he could sell on the street instead of take himself) and because (despite the sociopathic quality of his manipulation of welfare) he had good karma. In fact, he did build communities. They were, perhaps, not stable, but they encouraged socialization and reduced alienation. He collected people's food stamps (in violation of the existing rules) so that there were enough to buy nutritious food for everyone. He rescued runaways. He helped people in distress. And some of them were able to help him.

Soon after I saw him in the mental health clinic (and did not arrange for any drugs to be prescribed for him) a friend found him a place to live in an old house in the Haight district. The house was in probate following the death of its owner; a caretaker was needed to prevent vandalism. Harry soon filled that house with a community of S.S.I. recipients, burnt-out addicts, and down-and-outers. The lives of these people improved.

Because they paid little rent, what money they had could go further and be spent more wisely. Together they could afford good food; Harry loved to cook: especially baked chicken, steak, and shrimp. They could buy better quality recreational drugs—

usually marijuana, alcohol, and occasionally pharmaceutically produced speed—instead of the poor-quality and more dangerous street drugs they'd have been using otherwise. (Harry didn't allow IV drugs in the house, though he'd nurse an addict through withdrawal with a little Valium, care, and chicken soup.) And they had a place to live with other people who took an interest in them and who expected them to contribute to the welfare of the house. If they didn't contribute they wouldn't stay long. Harry made enormous messes when he cooked. The people he brought home were expected to clean up the kitchen and to provide a little affection and sex for their benefactor as well.

After the will was probated, they were forced to move to a much smaller place and things again got tumultuous. Barry's seizure disorder had become controllable only with so much medication that Barry's behavior was uncontrollable. He was becoming more of a burden than Harry could handle. But by then Harry had seen that a more stable life was possible. And partly through coincidence, he reestablished contact with the down and out kid of fifteen years ago, now the successful businessman in a position to help him. Harry's fortunes rose and fell a couple of times over the next few years. A couple of times he went back on welfare. His life-style was only partly compatible with the working and middle-class society into which he was moving. But his situation was improving. He was receiving the rewards for his good deeds.

Harry was fortunate, unlike many other Tenderloin residents, in having the likes of Toby and me take an interest in him, give him a perspective on his situation, and occasionally offer help. Perhaps, after all, Mary Baker Eddy had been right, and the positive thoughts were finally coming back.

Toby and I both learned from Harry. Perhaps the most important lesson was that each element of society has its own assumptions, values, ethics, and rules of conduct. Too often the dominant culture, believing its values and morals the only correct ones, imposes them on others. Too often it assumes that people who do not live its way are simply unable to, are the worse for it, and ought to acknowledge they are remiss. We discovered things are not so simple.

I'd been reared within the Roman Church. I'd come a long way in relaxing the self-righteousness and obsession with rules I'd learned as a child in Catholic schools, but it had never quite occurred to me that there were those who, without feeling in any way remiss, honestly believed my Christian values, especially regarding sex and relationship, wrong, anachronistic, pietistic, and even pathological.

I'd been raised among the middle class and my monastic training had taught me to value frugality and common sense in spending money. While I knew that the middle class sometimes overspent, especially the many nouveaux riches, I never thought people could believe that saving for the future was foolhardy, or that—because life offers the unexpected—delay of gratification was downright stupid, or that saving for old age was a waste of money that could neither provide security nor assure a long life.

I was a white American of British and Western European ancestry. I assumed that cleanliness was not only a good health practice, but a natural human inclination. I never expected to hear the remark, as I did from Barry, that he didn't like being around the agency where Toby and Harry worked because "the toilet is so damn clean, I just can't shit in there."

Harry's household taught me that while my values and sensibilities might represent those of the mainstream society and might even be reasonable and logical they weren't universal. My notions of politeness they sometimes took as effrontery. Though I must have seemed financially better off and, from my point of view, emotionally and sexually more mature, I couldn't really say I was that much happier or more fulfilled. In fact, I had a hard time answering Harry's accusations that I was just hung up and uptight. From my middle-class perspective Harry's life looked tumultuous and hysterical: he seemed always in one crisis or another. He told me my placidness looked dull and boring, while his life was vital and exciting.

I certainly couldn't claim that my middle-class values were any more correct than Harry's values. As a counterculturalist, first a monk and then an activist and hippie during the late '60s, I'd rebelled against the materialism of those values myself. I was certain that my parents' generation was not necessarily any happier or better off because they'd moved to the suburbs and acquired Cadillacs and boats. As a scholar of comparative religions, I'd seen through the trap of orthodoxy and dogmatism to recognize that truth is relative and plural: truth looks different from different perspectives. But I hadn't quite understood that this relativism and pluralism applied not only to philosophical and mystical thought, but even to issues as practical and routine as bathroom hygiene and sexual activity.

A major theme of Toby's *Politics of Homosexuality* is that just such a failure to recognize differing values and assumptions has been responsible for much of the suffering endured by conflicted homosexuals and even for the endless contention that took place among the various factions of the so-called liberated and liberationist-minded gay activists he was writing about.

According to his analysis, the first politically active homosexuals were influenced by the ideas of liberals and civil rights leaders: America should be a melting pot in which racial and ethnic differences disappeared; people should be judged according to things that really mattered, like intelligence, job competence, respectability rather than skin color, accent, or nationality. In the '50s and '60s, liberal-minded homosexuals applied these ideas to the case of sexuality, arguing that sexual preference was of little account and that it was unfair, unjust, and un-American to discriminate against individuals because they were homosexual. Hoping to deemphasize unconventional sexual practices, they referred to themselves not as homosexual but as homophile. Their main goal was to repeal laws that furthered discrimination on the basis of sexual orientation.

In 1969, during the heyday of the counterculture, liberationist-minded homosexuals adopted "gay"—the slang most active homosexuals used for themselves—as the name for their movement. Like the new term "black," gay signified supportive community, pride in difference, and determination to be recognized. The gay liberationists aimed less to change laws than to change consciousness. They called on individuals to take responsibility for their own lives, to seek self-actualization before social conformity, to be true to themselves, to speak their truth openly, and to respect others whose way of being true to themselves looked different. The mores of the counterculture, as applied to homosexuals, became the agenda for gay liberation.

The liberationists appealed not to heterosexuals but to other homosexuals. Be openly gay, they proclaimed. Come out and join the ranks of this movement of men and women who are aware of their difference and proud of it. It is in your own self-interest to be liberated. It doesn't matter what people think.

If only because of the way society forces them to learn about and conduct their sexuality—through secretive, transient intimacies—most homosexuals develop different assumptions about the role of sex in their lives. Sex takes on different meaning outside the context of marriage, reproduction, and child-rearing. Practices unconventional by traditional standards may make sense. Besides, many gay liberationists maintained, the most disturbing practices of homosexuals, like sex in public restrooms, are a result of oppression and internalized homophobia. The morality of homosexual lives can only be assessed from within the homosexual context. Difference and variety enrich society the counterculture said; conformity oppresses individuals and impoverishes society.

Respect for difference as well as self-actualization, Toby Marotta argued, was the key to "revolution through consciousness change." And belief in this new morality, not dope-smoking, LSD, long hair, blue jeans, rock music, free sex, or political dissent, was the essence of the counterculture and the corner-stone of liberationist politics.

By the end of the '70s, conservative social critics saw the counterculture not as a new morality, but as a set of fads and styles produced by a self-centered, narcissistic "me generation." If nothing else, Toby's research on gay life suggested that this was a jaundiced view. In both *The Politics of Homosexuality* and *Sons of Harvard,* he demonstrated that, thanks to the gay libera-tion movement and its popularizing the morality of being true to oneself and respectful of difference, the mental health, personal well-being, and social skills of homosexuals had dramatically improved. Indeed, by the end of the '70s, there had been a radical alteration not only in the way gay men and lesbians experienced themselves but in the way most Americans viewed homosexuals.

It was not that Toby didn't see that homosexuals, like every-one else, had a long way to go. The process of liberated life-style and community development is all very new, he admitted. People haven't entirely learned to be responsible for themselves and the consequences of their striving for self-actualization. People are just developing the notions of responsibility and obligation that can make self-expression the basis of an honest and humane society. And, unfortunately, in some people, and perhaps for many people at some stages, the countercultural call does result in self-centeredness, callousness toward others, and "narcis-sism."

Yet if the case of homosexuals is any measure, according to Toby, American culture is on the way to maturity. In that one very identifiable and visible group, a revolution in conscious-ness has been achieved, and more homosexuals are less neu-rotic and self-hating and more natural, satisfied, self-confident, and productive than they've been in recent history. "That's why I focused my research on such a controversial popula-tion," Toby once said to me. "The case is important because it shows how individuals of all kinds can get beyond their present situations."

The difficulty one person or one strata of society has understanding the sensibilities and motives of another is particularly acute in such areas as sexuality and religious piety. The result is often great confusion and misunderstanding.

Heterosexuals, for instance, often refuse to believe homosexuality really exists. They speak of it as a "phase." They assume that in same sex couples one person must play "the man," and the other "the woman." Suspecting that homosexual men (and perhaps lesbians) are simply giving in to temptations that all people feel to violate sexual restrictions, they jump to the conclusion that homosexuals obey no restrictions. Homosexuals, in turn, sometimes fail to acknowledge that heterosexuality really exists. They suspect that all people are repressed homosexuals.* They doubt that opposite sex couples can ever truly understand and respect one another.

The truth is that we all behave in ways that make sense to us. A prostitute, for instance, takes abuse from a pimp because that seems normal. A soldier in combat accepts the mission to murder because there is no alternative under the circumstances. The true believers in Jonestown drank the lethal Kool-Aid because in context it was the rational and socially acceptable thing to do for the promised salvation.

We may hope for a world in which there are no prostitutes, soldiers, or suicidal believers. But we'll certainly never achieve such a goal until we can understand the varied realities out of which their behavior arises and in which it seems perfectly natural.

Self-actualization implies not only being free but according that same freedom of self-expression to others. The challenge that faces those with such ideals is to learn responsibility for their

*The moralists' argument that homosexuality must be forbidden lest everyone turn homosexual and kill off the race seems to accept this peculiar assumption.

freedom, to learn that self-actualization is, in fact, not centered on "me." For what has to be liberated, what has to be actualized, is the ability to love.

The Wise Old Man and the Angel Guide—though, of course, neither of them thought of themselves as that—taught me that people live very different lives. What individuals need and value, what they expect and work for, varies greatly from person to person. There is no one way that everybody should be.

I understood that in principle, but it was really not until I left my comfortable, gentrified Noe Valley neighborhood and moved into the Tenderloin that I really saw how different people can be. I knew I was going to learn more than just sociological realities. I had been preparing myself for an heroic "adventure." I'd even told myself I was looking forward to a confrontation with the Lord of the Underworld—a necessary step, I knew, on the hero journey. Little did I know how unglamorous and how terrifying that confrontation was going to be!

THREE

The Truth About Juvenile Prostitution

The mythic hero is frequently portrayed as beginning his journey at night. This signifies that he begins in ignorance. And though he may have some idea of his goal, often he will be required to give up even that. What the hero discovers is that the truth of the everyday world is a self-perpetuating illusion. Behind the illusion is a deeper truth which he can only find in his own experience. In order to understand his experience he must face his own and the world's ignorance and confusion.

Just as Toby and I were beginning our fieldwork, the URSA staff regaled us with stories of hustlers found decapitated, young prostitutes thrown off high rooftops, and curious researchers "offed" by mobsters. I was frightened, but still enthusiastic.

The hotels we stayed in reeked of decay and death. Though they were slowly being refurbished by two young community activists who were trying to involve their tenants in the upkeep of their homes, the buildings were old and dilapidated almost beyond repair. These were not nice antiques, like so much of San Francisco, that needed only a little cleaning and polishing to shine with the splendor of a bygone age. New white paint could coat the surface, but underneath the paint the walls were saturated with pain and squalor. For too long these buildings had been tenements of hell.

The residents were old or enfeebled men and women who could afford no better or were those for whom alcohol had soothed away concern for something better, drag queens who performed in cheap dives nearby and enjoyed the toleration of their peculiarity in the neighborhood, junkies, chronic mental patients, black street toughs, and lost-looking teenage boys and girls. Some of the youth seemed at first bright and attractive, but in only a short time they turned dull and ordinary. The life in the neighborhood was culling the newcomers: those who had the looks or the intelligence or the breaks moved on; those who didn't got stuck.

There was a curious vitality about the place, however. There was constant activity. Partying and socializing went on day and night. Stereos played at all hours. People laughed raucously somewhere down the hotel hallway. Still, there wasn't much to do. The activity all seemed like a defense against boredom. I found I had a hard time concentrating. It was as though the collective mind of the whole neighborhood was bored, distracted, and despondent. There didn't seem to be anything else to do but get stoned and have sex.

I think for people like Harry Edwards who had lived in the neighborhood for years or for Ron and Hank, the activists who managed the hotels, the Tenderloin was just a location—albeit with its own rules and culture—that didn't interfere with the normal round of business and social life. But for newcomers, like the teenagers or like me, it was a state of consciousness.

That consciousness was acquainted with violence and death. Many local residents had criminal records. Law and order were not particularly cherished notions. "Getting by," "pulling a hustle" was the name of the game: "staying alive."

There was no simple story that everyone shared, no archetypal patterns. But the one thing most people had in common was that they'd had problems. And now they'd become problems for the rest of society. Of course, we were looking for teenagers involved in prostitution. We were expecting to find people with problems. And we did. But we found that the sex-related social problems were varied and complex.

Often a wide variety of sexual and social problems are lumped into simplistic categories. This blurs real differences among discrete individuals, attitudes, problems, and solutions. Some theories, for instance, hypothesize that teenagers turn to prostitution out of shame and inadequacy because of early sexual traumas or incest. Popular wisdom imagines children being recruited into the life by child molesters offering candy and drugs. We found such explanations fit only a small portion of the youth with whom we talked. Instead of simple, often repeated tales, we heard a multitude of unique stories.

We heard stories of kids who came from good families and got along with their parents. We heard stories of children driven out of their families by their Bible-thumping parents' religion and righteousness. We heard stories of girls thrown out for having a boyfriend and of boys thrown out for acknowledging homosexual experiences. We heard stories of broken families and multiple divorces and stories of solid, ideal nuclear families.

We talked with kids who had run away and with kids who were still living at home. We talked with those who hated what they were doing and dreaded each day and with those who were excited by the life and exuberant about the freedom and possibility they had found. Our field research and our statistics revealed that the sexual underworld is made up of varied subcultures, each with its own mores and values. The facts do not permit easy generalizations.

Frequently during the study I wondered if our own hypotheses and generalizations were self-perpetuating illusions. I'd seen in reviewing other studies and especially journalistic accounts that single cases, especially sensational ones, were generalized more than was warranted. And there was sometimes a curious circularity in the data: experts quoted each other as the source for the same findings. I wondered if we were guilty of a similar circularity, seeing only what we wanted to see, asking only the questions that would give us the answers we wanted. After all, in order to ask meaningful questions and to know if the questions are relevant, one must already know most of the answer. Even the most objective research can be circular, confirming its hypotheses by those very hypotheses or by the perspective they cause the research to take.

We chose the ethnographic approach to avoid the pitfall of circularity. Though we did gather statistical data from structured interviews conducted by personnel in agencies, we did not base our conclusions only on such forced-choice questionnaire responses or on statistical analyses of abstract data. We knew these could be self-proving. Instead we observed. We hung out in hotel lobbies and on street corners, talking informally with people on the scene. We joined the hustling subculture as far as we could without violating professional ethics or propriety. We did our best to remain open. We talked about our observations. We tried out different ways of understanding what we saw.

In fact, what we saw was that most of the hustlers are homosexual teenagers looking for ways to join the adult gay community. They want to learn what gay life is about. A little dazzled by the freedom offered, they're seeking models of how to live the new life they've discovered. These youth are members of the post-liberation generation. They have come out young. They have not gone through the years of alienation and confusion that previous generations of homosexuals had, wondering why their sexual feelings seemed different from those around them. They know, but that knowledge does not solve their problems. At least for the kids who end up on the streets, it seems to have replaced one set of problems with another. Having discovered their sexual orientation, they've searched out a gay community only to find there is little or no place in it for teenagers. And they've also found that in the cities, where most gay men are, jobs are hard to get and the cost of living is high. Nonetheless, in many cases because they stumble into households like that of Harry Edwards or into relationships with older gay men, most of the kids are surviving. To be sure, their lives are not easy. They are faced with dangers and obstacles, from beatings by sexually conflicted customers to the allure of drugs. But many of them said they were happy to have escaped their pasts and pleased that they'd found a community that understood their sexual feelings.

When I began to visit the youth agencies, I started to get a very different picture, though. We'd expected the social service professionals to have a jaundiced view. After all, they saw a select clientele: the youth most likely to seek social services were those having a hard time, the chronic losers, victims before they ever entered the street life, who became street people precisely out of that predisposition, and who continued to suffer its effects. We'd planned the field research to balance that bias. Besides, service providers had a vested interest in finding the scene unwholesome and in need of social service intervention. Nonetheless I knew the agency staff weren't lying to us just to protect their jobs.

The experts described hapless youths "used" sexually and discarded, exploited by older men, victimized and left to suicide or to mask their anguish with drugs and alcohol. They told me horrendous stories of kids raped and tortured and of innocent waifs seduced into relationships only to be thrown out a week or two later when the adult tired of them and brought home a new kid. But simultaneously they described the men who did this as weak adults with crippled personalities, driven to relate sexually with children because they had never grown up themselves and were terrified of adults. They told me stories of johns exploited and blackmailed by delinquent adolescents, caught in dependent relationships when they fell in love with a youth incapable of responding to adult needs. The stories didn't seem consistent with each other or with what we'd observed.

One agency director with very impressive credentials said to me, "I hope you're not relying on self-report for your data. You know, you can't believe a thing you hear from these kids or their customers." If we couldn't rely on self-report and we couldn't rely on experts' impressions, how could we find the truth? More than once I found myself in an epistemological dilemma.

I had indeed seen that some of the reports from the youth were exaggerated. Some of their stories were beyond belief. One youth claimed to be having sex for money sixty times a week. Perhaps extrapolating from one very exhausting day he could arrive at such a figure, but day after day it just didn't make sense. One teenage girl who identified herself as an S/M lesbian reported that she'd been kept by both a nationally known female sex symbol and a popular teen star (the developmental phases of whose heterosexual maturing are familiar copy in the *National Enquirer*). That these personalities were lesbian I could perhaps accept, but that this girl had by the age of seventeen been the S/M lover of both of them seemed unlikely. And the number of boys who reported having been paid for sex by a particular well-known TV comedian was incredible. The comedian seemed obviously homosexual: his caricature of himself comprised most of his appeal. But if, in fact, he'd been actually employing as many boys as my narrow sample suggested, he'd hardly have had time to make it to the television studio for his nightly appearances. The kids' claims to vast financial success, contact with movie stars, and extraordinary sexual prowess seemed obviously fabricated.

The reports of public officials, investigators, and supposed experts sometimes seemed equally confabulated. Expert data was inconsistent with facts. One large agency that appeals for contributions to save boys from homosexual prostitution kept no statistics on their clients' sexual behavior. They said that asking questions about such things would violate privacy and dignity, that it would be counter-therapeutic because it would bring up painful memories. For that reason they would not allow me to interview any of their clients. I accepted this rationale; I'd heard and believed it several times.

But when I spoke with a doctor who volunteers his time in their VD clinic, he said that of course he asks about sexual activity. How else could he know what to test for? And no, he said, the kids didn't seem upset. In fact, it was amazing how sophisticated about sex (if sometimes misinformed) and how unfazed about prostitution and homosexuality they all seemed. But less than 5 to 10 percent of the boys reported homosexual experiences, he replied to my question. That didn't correspond with the agency's public image.

On the street I heard that the boys warn one another away from this program because it's anti-gay and anti-sexual and because the delinquent non-gay youths who do go there make it dangerous for young effeminate boys. The agency doesn't seem to be performing the mission it thinks it is, or at least for which it is appealing for contributions. And it simply may not realize it isn't.

Reports from police were also conflicting. One officer, whom we were told was aiming for a high position in the Justice Department to spearhead a campaign against kiddie pornographers and pederasts, described all relations between youth and adults as sick and perverted. Declaring paradoxically that what the adults gave these youth was "L-O-V-E," he said the relationships would ruin the lives of these kids and leave them emotional cripples— kids who in the first place came from broken homes with little or no emotional support. On the other hand, an officer in a "runaway squad" said he didn't think the kids' sexual activity as much a problem as their parents' inability or refusal to accept and provide for them. He said he made friends with them and tried to help them out when he could. An officer in a "pedophilia squad" reported that his department practiced benign neglect, seeing that most of the kids took care of themselves pretty well. He said prostitution was part of society and they only stepped in when some real crime of violence was committed. Other officers reported that of course these kids aren't waifs and children, that they're in late adolescence, sexually precocious, and some of them pretty incorrigible. Most of them aren't having that much sex, they said; there are too many of them and too few customers. It's a buyer's market, the money is small, and only the good-looking kids are getting picked up.

Most of what the public knows about hustling comes from TV documentaries and journalistic pieces that focus on the horrors. (Good news seldom makes interesting viewing.) These are designed either to be sensationalistic or to motivate lawmakers to do something. Unfortunately little gets done, or what is done only worsens the situation. That is, at least in part, because the horror stories describe but a fragment of the scene. Legislators would have a very difficult time making comprehensive traffic laws if the *only* thing they knew about automobiles was that children are killed by hit-and-run drivers.

An investigative reporter described to me how eight-year-old boys are on sale for a thousand bucks a day by organized rings run by big crime syndicates who'll fly the kids wherever they're wanted. The kids are usually runaways who've been virtually kidnapped, imprisoned, and brainwashed. I was intrigued and upset by this. We hadn't uncovered anything of this sort. In fact, knowing it supposedly happened, we'd looked for it but had found no evidence. We'd presumed the incidents that occasionally made headlines were one-of-a-kind occurrences. But here was evidence. I wanted to know more. When I pursued the lead, asking to see the data, however, I was told by the reporter's boss that no further information would be released.

(Perhaps the boss was right in not releasing the data. The reporter had explained that he'd got his information by watching kids getting picked up along the meatrack in his city, taking down the license plate numbers of the cars, then contacting the johns and threatening to turn them in to the police and/or to expose them on television unless they would provide information. Data gathered under duress seemed of questionable value. Such testimony, after all, has been used to prove the existence of witches.)

I considered the reporter's story in light of information given me by a manager of "prostitution rings" of both males and females who had taken me into his confidence (though would never discuss whether any of his employees were under eighteen). He dismissed the whole idea of flying kids around for such large fees. "Nobody can pay that kind of money," he said, "there's practically a depression going on, you know."

About the recruitment process, he said he never had to recruit anybody and wouldn't want to: "You'd only be asking for trouble, especially with little kids. You can't trust them." His agencies did well enough employing the young men and women who came to them because they found that working for an agency was safer, easier, and more lucrative than free-lancing. "I know who they're with and where they are; if they don't call to check in when the time's up, I go out after them—with the police. My employees and my customers appreciate those sorts of assurances. I don't want anybody getting hurt. It's bad for business." And as for Mafia involvement, he only laughed, "This is penny-ante stuff, too easy to get burned for the little bit of money you can make."

The reports didn't jibe. But it was clear to me that nobody was really lying. The kids were describing their best-of-all-possible-worlds fantasies. As Fred Shick, a psychiatrist in Chicago who'd done a study of drug use among street kids and hustlers, explained, one appeal of the streets is that kids who've led hard or uninteresting lives get to scrap reality and make up their own histories. It gives them a feeling of control and choice over what they've never had any control or choice over before.

The social service agents, the police, and even the news reporters were describing real things they'd seen or were extrapolating from particularly horrendous stories they'd heard from youth, other service providers, or policemen. Most of them were still young, products of the liberal thought of the '60s, who wanted to do something to help society, to solve problems, to end suffering. Government programs, aggressive interventions that would stop the tragedies they'd occasionally seen, are necessary, they believe, if only for the sake of charity and decency.

Of course, just as the kids tell stories about their glamorous lives, in part, because that's what they think their customers— and certainly an author who might include them in a book— would want to hear, so they probably tell the social workers the stories they think *they'd* like to hear. They tell them about the time they got beat up, and maybe exaggerate the injuries. (In retrospect, we all seem to exaggerate our injuries from some accident or disaster.) They tell stories they've heard through the grapevine about other kids, and maybe let it sound like it's about them. They'll get sympathy that way—much more than if they talk about how good they've become at shoplifting since they aren't making much money hustling.

The police have heard similar stories, especially from kids who've wanted to make themselves look as innocent as possible. And police have found evidence. They've raided the homes of johns, for instance, and found snapshot collections of the hustlers the men have brought home. They have identified these snapshots as "kiddie porn" and hypothesized a network of photographers exchanging these photos. After all, the police are in the business of uncovering evidence and putting clues together to reveal what somebody else is supposed to be trying to conceal.

A man I interviewed told me he'd been driving home from work one night just after dark. At a busy intersection he saw a young man hitchhiking. Since it was getting late he picked him up. He usually picked up hitchhikers; he'd hitched himself and knew how frustrating it was to wait. Some people get hurt hitching, he said, so it's better for people like him to pick them up than leave them for the psychos. He knew he wasn't going to hurt anybody, and he'd never gotten hurt himself. Besides, occasionally he met a trick this way. Lots of gay guys hitchhike just to meet other men, he said. So do hustlers, and he wasn't above paying a hustler, especially if the guy was good-looking or really needed the money.

Not one to be bashful, after he'd made the routine small talk about where he was going and what the weather had been like, he announced to the hitchhiker that he was gay and said he hoped that wouldn't make the guy uncomfortable.

"Oh no," replied the hitchhiker. "Doesn't bother me. I go both ways myself."

"You've had sex with men?" said the man, beginning to think he'd made a lucky decision in picking up this fellow.

"Well, not a lot," the guy responded, but then went on to say he'd been fellated a couple of times and enjoyed it. That was the clue the man had been waiting for, he told me, and so he offered the proposition that the hitchhiker had clearly set up.

The proposition was accepted, though the hitchhiker hedged it by asking if the man had any marijuana. He liked getting high for sex. The man, taking that not only as a request for marijuana but as a statement of fee, said no he didn't have any grass. But he had twenty dollars he'd give the fellow to buy some.

The hitchhiker accepted the money but said he didn't know where to get grass right then. He suggested they forget about it and go on out to a place in the desert nearby. Seeing that the hustle had been successfully accomplished, the man happily drove on to where they could stop off the road without being noticed.

The fellow obviously enjoyed the sex, the man reported. He groaned and writhed all through it.

As he drove the guy home, the man asked if he might see him again. He'd enjoyed the sex too, even though it had been pretty one-sided. ("At my age and my weight," he said, rather more self-deprecating than was justified, "you take what you can get.") The fellow readily agreed to meet him the next night after he got off work from a fast food restaurant, reminding the man to try and score some grass.

The next night the man arrived at the time and place appointed. He hadn't brought any marijuana, but had some whiskey if the guy wanted to get high. He'd also brought along some lubricant in case the guy would be interested in taking an active role in anal intercourse. That way the man would get more sexual stimulation than just performing fellatio.

He saw the fellow inside cleaning the counters. In the light he looked younger than he'd thought him to be. But that didn't worry him. The kid had obviously known what he was doing and had enjoyed himself. After a longer time had passed than he'd expected, and wondering if the kid hadn't realized he was waiting in the parking lot, he got out of his car, walked over to the door, and peered in.

Just at that moment two policemen appeared behind him and announced that he was under arrest.

For reasons my interview subject never learned, the kid had turned him in. Maybe he'd been too late getting home or something, he suggested. He then showed me a copy of the testimony the youth, who turned out to be only seventeen, had given.

The youth reported that he'd been walking home from work when he saw a car following him at a distance. He'd become alarmed, tried to lose the pursuer by taking a detour, but had been unsuccessful. When he finally got to his house, he testified under oath, the man in the car had pulled up into the driveway, stuck his head out the window, and asked the youth if he "liked to play." When the youth responded, "Mister, I don't know what you're talking about," the man was reported to have said, "Well, I'll be waiting for you tomorrow night when you get off work."

The police, of course, believed the boy's story. They had no reason not to. They interpreted the evidence they found, a bottle of Jack Daniel's and a jar of Vaseline, as proof that the older homosexual intended to get the kid drunk and then commit sodomy on him.

My subject reported that he was lucky in some ways. Because the boy lied about the first night, he was charged only with solicitation and intent to commit a crime and not with statutory rape or some more serious offense. His lawyer, for a fee of a thousand dollars, got the charge reduced so that the man had only to plead guilty to a misdemeanor and pay the state another couple of hundred dollars.

This "crime" took place in Las Vegas, the center of vice in America where movie stars, friends of politicians, and racketeers of all sorts conduct an industry designed to appeal to prurient and greedy instincts. While the man I spoke with, of course, may have portrayed himself as more innocent than he was—though it's not clear what he could have admitted that would have been any more damning—it is a wonder that he could be prosecuted for his solicitation of vice in a city and state supported by vice. But it is no wonder that the police and the courts have a jaundiced and inaccurate view of the relationships, sexual and otherwise, between men and boys.

FOUR

Understanding
Juvenile Prostitution

The truth was elusive. Facts were hard to uncover. Understanding what the facts meant was made doubly difficult by the repeated use in the literature and by the experts we interviewed of certain "buzz words." For some of the people we spoke with and for the population at large, expressions like "exploitation," "sexual victimization," and even "male sexuality," stir visceral responses that have little to do with what the words denote or with what is actually going on.

The issues of sexual exploitation and victimization were raised throughout the study. It is in light of such notions that society prosecutes sexual transgressors and warns children of the dangers of "strange men." "Male sexuality" is sometimes said to be the root of these problems. Men are said to be unconcerned about whom they have sex with or how it is done, so long as it "gets them off." Studies of homosexual males who have had few committed relationships but thousands of sexual partners and of lesbians who have formed lasting, but sometimes almost asexual relationships, are offered as evidence of polar drives that characterize male and female psychologies and that attract heterosexual men and women to one another to balance the drives. Female sexuality, focused on affection and relationship, is thought to tame the male. Unbridled male sexuality is blamed for sexual victimization. This is, in part, why homosexual men—since their sexuality has, in theory, not been tamed by women—are thought of as perverts and child molesters. And this is how some radical feminists justify their objections to promiscuity, pornography, and to sex in general because it's all too "male." (Curiously, medieval Christians considered females to be wanton and sexually uncontrollable, while males, though subject to being led astray by females, were thought pure and innocent.)

When Michele Magee and I were in Minneapolis on a site visit, we had only a couple of days. We were trying to talk with as many people as possible. We were impressed with how much help was available in that city for the kids we were studying. But we were overwhelmed by the number of service providers we had to see. So when we were referred to Deborah Anderson, Director of the Sexual Assault Services Program of the Hennepin County Attorney's Office, we weren't sure we should follow up on the referral. We were investigating juvenile prostitution, not sexual assault. We'd seen those were two very different subjects, though we knew many people didn't distinguish them. We were concerned that a person in her position might be biased. But several people enthusiastically recommended that we speak with her, so we made an appointment.

At first Ms. Anderson seemed girlish and prim. She wore a dark, rather long dress with a collar closed tightly about her neck. Though she was attractive, she had affected the image of the thin-lipped, hard-as-nails, schoolteacher. I was expecting to hear the same derision of sex I'd heard before. But as she began to speak, her manner relaxed, she became quite animated, and the schoolmarm image disappeared. Perhaps she'd been expecting Michele and me to be moralistic graduate students or journalists looking for sensationalistic stories and had prepared herself to be aloof.

As she warmed to us and to the subject, I realized hers was the most intelligent discussion I'd yet heard of sexual victimization. She had worked with children who had been victims of sexual assault and with adults who had perpetrated such acts. In a way that most social workers and youth agency personnel had not, she'd seen both sides of the issue. Of course, it was a huge topic, she explained, and she could only begin to scratch the surface. But in her job she'd seen that it was badly misunderstood and she was eager to share her insights.

There are actually not two sides to it, victim and victimizer, she began. The perpetrators of sexual abuse of children are adults who themselves had been victims as children. They are simply repeating behavior they learned in childhood. Their victims are generally children of parents who have been victims, and most often the victimizers are the parents themselves. Sexual abuse runs in families.

There are molesters outside the family, of course. But even they often pick children from families of victims. Sexual abuse victims and victimizers pick one another out, she suggested, as if by radar. What seems to happen is that parents who have been victims develop faulty attitudes that deny sexuality. They convey this denial to their children who then also develop faulty attitudes and, therefore, lack the good sense to avoid dangerous situations.

Most children know not to follow a stranger into a dark alley to look for a kitten, she offered as an example. But a child whose sense of sexual danger is distorted will go right into the alley. The very repugnance of sex the parent has conveyed renders the child blind to the danger. The molesters also are denying the reality of their actions; they are still repeating their own childhoods. They've become no more able to see what they're doing than they were when *they* followed the stranger into the alley or acquiesced to the sexual advance of a parent.

Denial is the major dynamic of this cycle. Frequently, a victim of sexual abuse learns to deny the sexual feelings involved, especially if the molester or incestuous parent is criminally prosecuted, because the child is left to feel responsible for the event or for the subsequent breakup of the family. And, unfortunately, the terror of child molestation society generates in the hopes of protecting children perpetuates the denial. For in children who've already inherited the victim attitude and in those who've grown up and are becoming victimizers, the condemnations and warnings tend to force further from mind the reality of what they're getting into.

What has to be done, Ms. Anderson said, is to break the cycle of denial. It is possible to screen families to determine those in which the victim/victimizer messages are likely to be conveyed. The Minneapolis public schools were experimenting with doing just that. Parents can be helped to recognize how they pass on the denial patterns. Once the victim role has been eliminated there'll be fewer victimizers.

I didn't understand this idea of denial at first. Was she suggesting that child molesters aren't conscious when they're lurking in dark alleys waiting for children or when they're offering drugs to a ten-year-old as a bribe for sex or a damper on inhibitions?

Perhaps it isn't quite that they're not conscious, she answered, but that they're interpreting the experience in ways that to them seem less sexual and less negative.

Denial is a powerful mechanism in the psyche. We are all familiar with it. We all do it. We all think "it won't happen to me." When we smoke a cigarette, thinking we won't get cancer, or fail to fasten our seatbelts in the car, we're in denial. And when we call things by different names in order to avoid facing their reality, we're in denial.

The things we ignore or prefer not to see are still there: that funny noise in the car's steering mechanism, that lump in our body. Our unconsciousness of them only makes them unmanageable. Things we deny and repress into the unconscious still affect our behavior; we are just not conscious of them. They may become the source of blind emotions or uncontrollable compulsions we cannot understand.

Children may not be told about sexual feelings, but they don't become less sexual. Instead they may deny the feelings, feel guilty, and become compulsively sexual without even quite knowing that what they're doing is sexual. Denial does not solve problems. Indeed, in a curious way, things and conditions we value negatively, resist, and deny tend to be confirmed in the external world. The resistance seems to create a self-fulfilling prophecy.

In *The Family Book About Sexuality,* Mary Calderone suggests that teaching a child to deny sexual feelings is a kind of child abuse. A history of such abuse may be what keeps individual kids from recognizing what's happening to them in the sexual underworld, keeps the girls from realizing how badly they're being treated by their pimps, and keeps already conflicted boys from recognizing the homosexual component of their activity. The denial keeps them confused and weakened. They fail to recognize danger, take too many drugs, make poor decisions, and occasionally go off with the wrong john who will beat them or kill them.

Indeed, throughout society, sex-negative attitudes may cause basic sexual urges to be confused with perverse sexual behavior, like rape, incest, and child molestation, or with socially reprobated forms of sexual behavior, like promiscuity, homosexuality, prostitution, sado-masochism, or such problems as venereal disease and sexual dysfunctions. This confusion may be in part responsible for the occurrence of such things. The condemnation of sex may create the very problems it is trying to stop.

Another buzz word was "exploitation." It is unclear what the word means. The way many people use it regarding sexually active teenagers seems to assume that teenagers do not enjoy sex, are forced into it only by adults or by circumstances, and are somehow hurt by it. The first assumption is patently untrue. The second is only partly true. Youth who have no jobs and no supports are going to seek money any way they can; thus, hustlers can be said to be forced into demanding money for sex and perhaps into being less discriminating about how and with whom they have sex. And the third assumption is not necessarily true. Sex itself doesn't have to cause harm; what probably causes more harm is confusion about sexual identity, misgivings and guilt about sex, and poor relationships within which that sex takes place.

Sexual activity, of course, can be *defined* as harmful. That is partly how teenage male prostitution becomes classed as exploitation: because sex (especially homosexuality) and promiscuity have been declared sinful by religion, they are considered harmful. This definition, however, based to some degree on a denial of male sexual urges, itself causes harm, for it contributes to confusion, misgivings, and guilt.

Both the boys and the johns we spoke with agreed that if there is exploitation—in the usual sense of taking advantage of someone—it is most often of the adults by the hustlers. It is the kids who extort or steal from the adults. Many of the teenage girl prostitutes are exploited, but much less by the sex they are experiencing than by the pimps who play on their naive and distorted notions of love and male-female relationships and their confusion about the real urges they feel in their bodies.

One observer I spoke with defined exploitation as "setting conditions for acceptance and love." A john exploits a hustler, he explained, when he says, "I will support you and keep you off the streets only if I can fuck you." But if setting conditions is what makes for exploitation, he added only half facetiously, then the parental relationship is the most exploitative.

Of course, what is most commonly meant by sexual exploitation is the production of pornography. The common wisdom has been that taking photos of children's bodies turns them to prostitution. But despite our efforts we could not find any hustlers who'd been photographed as children. That may mean that the experience was so traumatizing no one would come forth. More likely it means the production of kiddie porn and juvenile prostitution don't have much to do with one another, and so among hustlers there wasn't much experience of being photographed for kiddie porn. No one among our subjects reported being drawn into prostitution by a pornographer.

In our research we tried to find kiddie porn. The only examples we could find of mass-produced kiddie porn were all made before 1977, and in what we found almost all of the subjects, while young, were postpubescent. We were told by bookstore owners that such materials were simply no longer available through the open market. Legislation following congressional hearings on "sexploitation" effectively curtailed production in the late '70s. (Ironically, the bookstore owners explained that S/M porn appeared about that time to replace kiddie porn. I wonder if the photos of innocents in vaguely provocative poses were not, in fact, much less likely to stimulate dangerous and antisocial fantasies than pictures of sexual athletes trussed up in black leather whipping one another.)

We did speak with some teenagers and young men who'd been photographed. Most reported the pictures had been Polaroid photos taken as souvenirs by johns whom they'd met hustling. We also met some men who'd been subjects for mass-produced pornography (one of them, in fact, was director of an agency I visited). I was surprised by their report of the experience. They spoke proudly of the first-class photographic job. They found the production crew positive, supportive, and understanding. No one pressured them. They enjoyed themselves. They felt appreciated and personally affirmed. No one felt dirtied by the experience. These men were photographed for gay pornography; the sex depicted was between equals; the objections frequently posed by feminists that pornography "exploits" women because it appeals to male, visually-triggered sexuality and often depicts women as powerless victims simply were not applicable. And, of course, these men were adults. Their experience may be quite different from that of women or of younger, less experienced people.

I do not mean to say that there is no such thing as exploitation, but that it is difficult to define in the abstract. And the use of words like victimization and exploitation obscures the issue. Any two people use and are used by one another. It should only be called victimization or exploitation when one takes unfair advantage of the other, and when one is hurt by the other. And I do not mean to say that no one is hurt in the prostitution world. There is a degree of callousness, violence, and drug use that certainly warps personalities and creates individual tragedies. Children are sometimes forced into behavior they simply cannot understand. But the connections between the young prostitutes and their adult customers are not necessarily always unfair or hurtful. In fact, they can be beneficial in ways that the jargon makes impossible to consider.

FIVE

The Findings on Juvenile Prostitution

Toby stayed in the Tenderloin for nearly a year. Because my job was going to be the review of service agencies, I moved back home to Noe Valley after three months. Still I spent most of my days, when I wasn't doing paper work at URSA, roaming the Tenderloin and nearby Polk Street, another prostitution area we studied.

Then in the fall we made visits to a number of cities around the country. By the time the study was over, URSA personnel had visited New York, Boston, Houston, Los Angeles, Minneapolis, Seattle, Muncie, and Charleston, South Carolina. Toby and I and other members of the URSA team had spoken with hustlers, johns, police, social workers, hotel managers, cafe owners, business people, city officials, and neighborhood regulars.

Through such interviews with as many people as possible (and it was surprising how many different kinds of people had had some firsthand experience with prostitution and were eager to report their impressions), through observation, and through discussion with other observers and experts, we refined and validated our understanding. By the end of twenty months, we had some solid findings.

The findings seem almost obvious, though in fact they are at odds with most "conventional wisdom" and "official opinion." Simply stated they are:

1. Juvenile prostitution, the production of kiddie pornography, child molestation, incest, and child abuse, while sometimes overlapping, are distinct sexual social phenomena that must be analyzed separately.

2. Male and female prostitution are radically different. Mainly because the former primarily involves homosexual behavior while the latter almost exclusively involves heterosexual behavior, different psychological and social dynamics are involved. Some males prostitute to females, but they are few, and probably cannot depend on heterosexual activity alone to support themselves.

3. There are probably more teenage boys in prostitution than teenage girls.

4. The males involved in prostitution are generally older than popularly imagined. Most are in the range from age 17–23. While there may be some very young "boys for sale," the number is small. They represent an individual criminal problem, but not a significant social problem.

5. Different types of male prostitutes have different experiences, self-perceptions, and service needs. The key to understanding the hustlers is to see that those involved in what we identified as prostitution view themselves and their participation in the trade in a variety of ways. Unless one understands their different self-perceptions, one cannot correctly assess their problems and needs.

Overall, the self-perceptions of girls involved in prostitution seem closer to the popular stereotypes than do those of the boys, though as female prostitution catches up with the sexual revolution the familiar notions are becoming obsolete. While we did not do our own research into juvenile female prostitution, we got reports from other researchers, the boys, and the collateral sources, and in the agencies I talked with staff and with a few girls who'd been involved in prostitution.

The most striking difference between male and female prostitution is the involvement of adult male pimps. This seems directly connected to the females' self-perceptions and attitudes. Paradoxically, young female prostitutes frequently have traditional moral standards and life expectations. Some believe one day they'll marry and raise a family. They think that their proper place is with a man. Thus many attach themselves to a dominant male with whom they feel they are in love. Sometimes these men are indeed lovers; they too may be hustling to survive. But other males do little more than manage their "girlfriends' " earnings. Often such pimps maintain relationships with several females simultaneously. They refer to these women as their "stable." (In a curious way, the girls might be said to be in monogamous relationships with their pimps. They "make love" only with them. They have sex with johns in order to earn money for their pimps to prove their love. They sometimes feel it's "cheating" to have sex for pleasure with another man.)

Some girls seem to get along pretty well with their pimps. But others endure an enormous amount of abuse: they are overworked, beaten, and kept emotionally frustrated. In keeping with their expectations of traditional marriage, they may see this abuse as consistent with the role of wife. It is often quite difficult for the police to prosecute pimps because their girls refuse to testify against them.

Some observers theorize that because these girls have been victimized as children, often being incest or rape victims, they feel no sexual self-worth and so do not resist the obvious maltreatment. Perhaps the explanation is slightly simpler and less psychiatric than that. The girls' attitudes seem less the results of traumatic experiences than distorted exaggerations of conventional womanly roles. Because they do, indeed, frequently come from violent and distressed families, they may have learned to expect the relationship between a man and a woman to be tinged with terror. Their mothers feared and took abuse from husbands and lovers, and they themselves, as victims of incest or simply as daughters, feared and took abuse from fathers or older brothers.

The boys seldom have pimps. Some of them have "lovers,"

other boys or occasionally girls, whom they support, but the relationships are rarely that of prostitute-pimp. The teenage boys do not appear as needy and dependent as the girls and as likely to fall into such victimizing relationships. Many of them, either in distressed families, institutions, or group and foster homes, have become emotionally independent of parents and disciplining adults very early. While some of them come from very troubled backgrounds, our survey, compared with that of studies of girls, indicated that the boys haven't had the same frequency or degree of abuse—physical, sexual, emotional—as the girls.*

Most youth become involved with prostitution out of immediate needs—for income, for excitement, for affection and support. Some of these are teenagers who come to the city with no money and nowhere to live. Some are troubled, having run away from intolerable backgrounds where they've been emotionally, physically, and perhaps sexually abused. They are often looking for some kind of help, though they may be unable or afraid to ask for it directly. Others are the young men who've come to find other homosexuals. Sometimes they have no intention of selling sex and are surprised when one of the men they've picked up gives them a $20 bill. They learn from experience or from other youth that sex can be a commodity. When their situation improves, because they find a job, get some kind of financial aid, or find someone who'll take them in, they will usually stop hustling. These we categorized as "situational hustlers." Such situational hustling is almost always the point of entry into male prostitution.

*Sexual abuse of boys is much more indefinite than of girls. A mother simply can't rape a son the way a father can rape a daughter. Most homosexual advances amount to fondling, not penetration, and a boy will likely find fondling pleasurable. What creates the trauma of sexual abuse for both boys and girls is often less the sex than the adults' anxiety and insistence on secrecy and the threats if the child reveals what happened.

There are also young men, often no longer teenagers, who have discovered they can make good money hustling. They identify as hustlers and consider prostitution a job. Some of them recognize the occupational hazards and take care of their bodies, avoid abuse of drugs, and plan for future careers. These we categorized as "vocational hustlers."

Some young men who have jobs have found that prostitution is an easy and exciting way to supplement their income. Some of them hope to meet influential people. The very attractive and personable among them can appeal to a rich and powerful clientele who may help them with their careers. (One man I spoke with is a doctor who'd paid his way through medical school by part-time prostitution.) These were "avocational hustlers."

Some of the hustlers become dependent on hustling. They've lost interest in working regular jobs and survive by exploiting the world. Drugs, alcohol, the fast life, poor self-image, and alienation from society have left them unable to cope with life. They become chronic welfare recipients, petty thieves, down and outers, and derelicts. This is generally the dead end of hustling. These were "habitual hustlers."

Both vocational and avocational hustlers, conscious of their intention to prostitute, work free-lance, frequenting "hustler bars" and advertising in the gay or swingers' press as models or masseurs. They may also work through agencies which, for a commission, handle advertising and assignations. Of course, they often develop a regular clientele.

Situational hustlers, just starting out with little experience and often unrealistic but optimistic expectations, and habitual hustlers, now going off the deep end with few expectations at all, work primarily free-lance, usually from the street or in bars if they can get in. Because they're less intentional about prostitution, their "hustle" is of a much broader sort. They take what they can get. Sometimes that means taking money for sex and sometimes it means thievery. Situational and habitual hustlers may hang out side by side on the same "turf." But in major cities they tend to frequent distinct areas.

In many cities, and even in small towns, there is an area, usually in a run-down part of the downtown, characterized by businesses catering to sexual interests. In such "sex-trade zones" are the porno houses, "dirty bookstores," sex-appliance shops, massage parlors, saunas, encounter parlors, and night clubs through which sex and sex-for-fee can be found.

These neighborhoods are generally shabby, many of the buildings abandoned and ramshackle. Those who live in the area are often drug users, criminals, veterans of the sex industries, and the urban poor—the elderly, the refugees new to America, the mentally ill, the lackadaisical. The businesses are those that cater to the poor: secondhand stores, corner grocery and liquor stores, bars, transportation terminals. The residents live in run-down hotels and hang out in the lobbies or on the sidewalks. Crime of all sorts goes on, from petty theft to hard drug trafficking to organized murder and arson. These are the parts of town into which people can disappear (and in which they sometimes do disappear). For that reason they've been the refuge for fugitives—many of whom are the youth who've run from home, come to the cities by bus, and been let out there. For that same reason they were the first neighborhoods to permit the creation of bars, baths, and other institutions catering to homosexual men.

At almost all hours of the day and night, women and men and girls and boys can be found walking the street or leaning up against lampposts willing to be drawn into conversation, sometimes even aggressively pursuing it. Usually within the zone is an even smaller area, a corner, a block, perhaps a mini-park, or bench at a known bus stop, that is the "meatrack." Here the boys, and sometimes their girlfriends, are available for pick up.

What characterizes a sex-trade zone is the anonymity of the

area and of the interactions of the denizens. Anything goes. Nothing about the area makes it specifically homosexual. This is important, for it means that the area is comfortable for those men and teenage boys who are not comfortable with homosexual sex, even though they might engage in it routinely and regularly. Some hustlers find that taking money for sex allows them to deny the homosexual implications of their behavior. For many the sex-trade zone is a populated and titillating but secure closet. Examples of such sex-trade zones are San Francisco's Tenderloin, New York's Times Square, and Boston's Combat Zone including Park Square.

For a new generation of homosexuals who openly and proudly call themselves gay, the anonymity and sleaze of the sex-trade zone is unappealing, though. In recent years, these liberated homosexuals have clustered not in the sex-trade zones but in identifiably gay communities developed in urban neighborhoods. In most cases, these gay neighborhoods have resulted from the "geriatrification" and subsequent "gentrification" of run-down residential districts as gay entrepreneurs have invested in real estate, remodeled old homes, and opened businesses for other gays.

The gay neighborhoods are usually attractive and affluent, with shops catering to gay tastes in clothing and furnishing, and with bars and restaurants catering to gay social styles. Those living in these areas are usually gay people who have moved there to find supportive and non-threatening neighbors and the older residents who predate the shift in neighborhood complexion and remain because they cannot afford to move or because they feel safer among gay men than among a mixed urban population more likely to contain delinquent youths who prey on the aged. These neighborhoods have been referred to as "gay ghettos" in the sense that they offer gay men (and sometimes, though to a lesser extent, lesbians) a comfortable but contained environment, free from disapproving gazes, in which to be openly affectionate (and sometimes—even under the disapproving gazes of other homosexuals who may feel things are going too far—openly sexual).

Gay neighborhoods sometimes develop within high-class, historical, or artsy neighborhoods. Bars, restaurants, and shops cater to wealthy and urbane homosexuals. This can create a cruising atmosphere in the area which attracts young men seeking the favors of these wealthy homosexuals. But the neighborhood is not gay-identified.

Examples of the first type of gay neighborhood are New York's Christopher Street and San Francisco's Polk and Castro Streets; and of the second type New York's 53rd Street and Third Avenue and parts of Los Angeles' West Hollywood.

Gay neighborhoods are characterized by the "fast life"—action-packed, fun, self-indulgent. Some residents have the intelligence and self-knowledge to retreat periodically from that life to a more peaceful home and work life. Others get caught exposing themselves to psychological and, it has recently been discovered, physiological hazards. These men who pursue the life-style to the hilt have come to be known as "clones." The clone life, with its distinctive look and virile attractiveness may appeal to youth, new to the city and looking for adventure, who often may not be particularly perspicacious in their choice of models.

The gay neighborhoods certainly attract youth. Many of them are relieved to find there are environments, unlike their hostile families, where they can express burgeoning homosexual feelings. Eager to enter gay life, they are sometimes perplexed because all its institutions are restricted to adults. Some are discovering they can exploit their youth and good looks and, in return for sex, get adults to provide them money, goods, services, and opportunities.

Most of those who frequent such areas are gay. Some of them feel themselves "sexual revolutionaries," violating taboos in the name of freedom and adventure, out to indulge in the sexual activity that had been forbidden elsewhere. Some adults easily spend a portion of their largesse on a sexual encounter to fulfill a fantasy. And some youth "put out" to make a little money, have sex, feel appreciated, and find a place for themselves in the subculture.

Some of these, especially the youngest of them, may not be fully gay-identified; they may still be questioning and confused. Yet they may find they have no other income and soon lose control of their need to seek adults who'll pay them for sex. Some may have traumatized pasts which they continue to act out by bringing on themselves further and even more threatening traumas because they cannot resolve serious issues of personality development.

Some of the adults may resort to sex with hustlers because they no longer feel attractive to peers, because they are "burnt out" on cruising and want to have sexual urges taken care of as efficiently as possible with the least threat to their character structure, or because they find adolescents both sexually appealing and refreshing.

What makes the area a gay neighborhood is the open, perhaps defiant, gay identification of the habitués. Prostitution in the gay neighborhood is different from that in the sex-trade zone. Customers are likely to live, or be staying in hotels, nearby and to bring the youth home with them and to be less secretive in their dealings with them. The youth are more likely to be gay and, because they don't live in the same ambience of illegality as do those in the sex-trade zone, less likely to be criminals.

The hustlers who work in the sex-trade zones appear by far the more conflicted about sexuality and the more dependent on prostitution. Similarly the johns in the sex-trade zones appear the more conflicted. They have gone to that part of town *because* of its clandestine quality. They are not looking to meet someone refreshing, but to pay for anonymous sex. The habitual hustlers end up in the sex-trade zones, while the situational and vocational tend to gravitate away from them toward the gay neighborhoods. The revolution through consciousness change that produced the gay neighborhoods, making gay life so much more positive for the new generation of homosexuals, also changed the nature of hustling, making it less dangerous, degraded, and destructive.

We were asked to make recommendations for government interventions. Partly in the spirit of the popular mandate, evidenced in the 1980 elections, to curtail government interference in private lives and partly in the spirit of our own countercultural libertarianism, Toby and I worked to devise recommendations that made sense in a time of limited expenditures on social services. Working in a hospital emergency room where services are realistically limited had convinced me of the wisdom of triage: there is no need to help those who'll survive without help or who are already past the point of help.

The situational hustlers who are simply "sowing wild oats," playing with new-found freedom until they tire of the fast life and take a sensible job, get a lucky break, or develop a relationship with someone who'll provide an adult role model and the opportunity to finish school or begin a career, don't need services. The vocational and avocational hustlers who make good money and take care of themselves don't need services (other than warnings about pitfalls and, perhaps, sound investment advice).

Moral and religious groups, of course, may want to "save" even those who don't *need* social services, though they may find they'll do more harm than good. And gay community groups may want to welcome the youth into the gay community through teen social and rap groups and to try to protect them from the dangers they face (and there are some real dangers).

The habitual hustlers who started out as situational, but whose situations either never changed or got worse, and the vocational and avocational who ignored the occupational hazards or fell on hard times and never got on their feet again—these are the youth who need social services to prevent further social problems: crime, vandalism, and welfare costs. But they need the help *before* they ever fall into the habitual category, for once there they are very difficult to retrieve.

The question is how to determine who is in the middle group of those who won't survive without help—that is, how to determine which youth will slip from one of the stable and self-limiting categories into the habitual category. That became the major issue in developing our recommendations for societal interventions.

It appeared from our statistics, our interviews, and the reports given us by our other sources that among the factors that predisposed youths to fall into the habitual category were:

1. a low-life background, so that they never expected to become self-sufficient;
2. a history of severe abuse (including sexual) during childhood;
3. sexual identity confusion, so that in spite of their behavior, the boys insisted they were not homosexual and the girls that they would one day marry and raise normal families; and
4. a history of arrest or institutionalization.

The first two are obvious and expected. But they are past history that can't be changed by agencies serving adolescents. Dealing with economic inequity and child abuse require vast changes in our economic system and in our patterns of child rearing. The latter two, on the other hand, are surprising. And they can be dealt with in the present. The first two factors affect who is screened in for intensive services. The second two affect how these services are given.

Most social service providers encourage youth to think of themselves as "normal," with all-American futures still ahead of them. But encouraging "normality" only seems to compound denial.

The great majority of male teenage hustlers identify themselves as gay. Since many gay men have hustled, if only briefly or for a lark, there is little or no stigma attached. Some adults are interested in developing relationships with these youth. And jobs in gay-owned enterprises are available that do not require a boy to deny his past. But some boys can't accept the gay identification and insist they're straight, thus excluding themselves from the major means of exit from hustling. Yet in mainstream American society, a male who, except in a rare homosexual "experiment," has had sex with another male— regardless of the style—is "queer." Besides, despite their insistence that they "prefer girls" and that "guys don't really turn them on," male sexual response is such that a truly repugnant situation simply would not arouse them. Boys who are truly heterosexual will find the homosexuality so difficult that they'll find other means of support. Dealing dope is just as easy a way to make money as hustling, just as available, and no more illicit.

Girls who've prostituted have a much harder time than boys. There is stigma in heterosexual society. Employers are reluctant to hire a young woman who reports she's been a whore for the past three years. Few men really want to marry such a woman. Her efforts to pursue normality are blocked in every direction. Perhaps those women who develop strong feminist identities and reject the traditional wifely role may develop the self-confidence to build their own lives. At any rate, while, of course, most of the girls do seem heterosexual, those who discover themselves lesbian or who react to their prostitution experience by choosing to live independent of men seem to adjust well. Of the ex-hookers I met, those who had made the most satisfactory adjustments were the feminists and the lesbians.

The social service agencies—and society in general—ought to consider carefully what kind of expectations they want to give these youth. The youth would do better if they were given realistic and adaptive self-images rather than being "normalized" and rehabilitated.

While police officers themselves believe that they are only enforcing laws, the general presumption is that arrest and punishment is a deterrent to crime and, at least with youth, an occasion for rehabilitation. But arrest or institutionalization only further alienates youth from society. Rather than being deterred from crime, they seem only more likely to be condemned to it. Youth who are arrested for prostitution and sent back to the homes they've run from feel resentful, angry, and powerless. Those who are incarcerated or sent to juvenile halls become buddies with kids who've committed serious crimes like robbery and murder. They become socialized into a life of crime. It has become a commonplace that jails and prisons are schools for criminals. This is especially true for youth.

Police departments are often a stumbling block to resolving problems of juvenile prostitution in other ways as well. This is not the fault of individual officers: almost all of the police we spoke with were understanding, well motivated, and interested in learning facts that could help them do better by the kids. The problem is that the police as an institution responds to public pressure. The roots of crime and civil disorder are complex and poorly understood. Public pressure is often not concerned with what is done, so long as *something* is done. A few weeks before an election, for instance, apparently in the interests of getting the religious vote, police are sent out by politicians to "clean up the streets." Even though it may be counterproductive, they enforce society's prejudices and misunderstandings.

Law enforcement agencies, and the society that believes in law and order and sends the police on its missions, ought to consider carefully what kinds of interventions they want to make. A meeting of service providers in the Tenderloin drafted a letter to the San Francisco chief of police arguing that the juvenile prostitutes would do better if police tried to protect them from crime and refer them for public assistance rather than harrass or arrest either them or the adults who provide them an income.

But social services do try to rehabilitate the youth and reunite families so everyone gets back to "normal" and the police do arrest the youth. Thus, while of course some (situational) kids *are* saved, it looks as if society's main interventions may push the problem youth into habitual hustling. Is there no solution?

SIX

The Solution to Juvenile Prostitution

If there is a solution to the problem of juvenile prostitution, it may be to reconsider what the problem really is. At least to some extent this may help to break the cycle of denial. The real problem, and almost every service provider I spoke with reiterated this, is homelessness and joblessness, not promiscuous or illicit sex.

What is most visible in juvenile prostitution are the teenage boys, who hang out on the streets, apparently waiting to get picked up, socializing with one another, occasionally hawking joints or street drugs, sometimes getting rowdy and committing acts of vandalism and petty theft. Some of them are unpredictable and dangerous—to themselves and to others. The presence of these street kids often frightens tourists and shoppers and can create a nuisance for local businesses.

Because hustling sex is the main source of income for most of them, the problem is often referred to as a problem of prostitution. This is misleading. Prostitution is usually understood as payment for sexual services to a woman who is working for a pimp or madam. This is simply not the case for most of these street kids. Most are boys working independently, seeking sex and adventure as much as they are money.

The problem for society and for the youth themselves is much less a problem of prostitution or "sexual exploitation" than one of the presence in urban areas of independent, jobless, sexually precocious teenagers for whom there is little place in mainstream society. Such a problem is not new; there have always been such youth, both male and female. But their numbers and their visibility have increased in recent years. And society's ability to assimilate them seems to have decreased.

A major block to resolving these problems is teenage unemployability. But unemployment is more complex than simple job availability. The hustling life is more lucrative and exciting, permitting a great deal more freedom and adventure, than most jobs open to teenagers. The decision to work must be based on some sense of responsibility to oneself or to another. (That is why the youth given a job by a john or a "sugar daddy" is probably more likely to keep it than the job assigned by a government agency.) The jobs the kids might take will have to be attractive and interesting if they're going to compete with hustling.

Young hustlers and hookers are certainly not the only jobless teenagers. Teenage unemployment is one of the worst problems in American society. Prostitution is only one small consequence. Much worse than illicit sex is the violence that many teenagers commit because they feel bored, alienated, and angry. The number of robberies and senseless shootings by teenagers is increasing, particularly among black youth who have special reason for feeling angry and disenfranchised. Actually the prostitutes are less a problem than the hoodlums. They do have a sort of job and they don't necessarily hurt other people. The best way to prevent youth from becoming habitual prostitutes is to provide those who want them ways of becoming self-respecting and self-supporting.

There are agencies trying to redefine the problems in ways that can be dealt with. Unfortunately they are probably too few and their interventions ineffective. This is less because existing agencies are inept than because they are caught in a contradiction between what their own personnel may recognize as needed and what the society will allow them to do. Few public agencies feel free to support gay-identified youth in that sexual orientation. How much less free they feel to convince panicky "straight" hustlers that they should identify as gay.

Most of the shelters for runaways are committed to the government's policy of family reunification. But the families were often the source of the original problems. And, besides, since many young prostitutes have moved physically or emotionally far away from their families, reunification is often not only undesirable, but impossible. As a result, many agencies simply don't work with these youth. But all the agencies in the country won't solve the problems, no matter what tack they take. The problems of teenagers are intertwined with the problems of all of American society and of modern life itself.

As a society, we do not pay attention to the consequences of our attitudes about sexuality, homosexuality, pederasty, prostitution, or pornography. We do not see that our attitudes and misconceptions could contribute to our problems.

I could understand how the misperceptions of juvenile sex arise. I recalled my own inabilities as a youth to acknowledge openly my sexual experience, as solitary and sequestered as it was. I could understand how parents could have a difficult time seeing their children's maturing into a world of sexual behavior so different from that of their own youth. I could understand how a few highly sensationalized events like the killing of young girls or the mass murder of boys could create a sense of terror, especially when they were connected with such maligned and poorly understood phenomena as homosexuality and prostitution. I could understand how police, social workers, and other members of the social establishment could develop honestly-held but incomplete views. And I could even understand how such views were perpetuated and sensationalized by the news media which, after all, really only feed people what they want. But they are misconceptions nonetheless. Ignorance and error are self-perpetuating; they create self-fulfilling prophecies. Only by resolving the misconceptions can the problems be resolved.

Common sense tells us that force and punishment are bound to stop people from doing things we don't like, and so we do not reward positive behavior nearly as much as we try to punish the negative. But, paradoxically, punishment often works as a reinforcement. The rules that govern life just don't seem to obey the principles of common sense. Creating ever harsher penalties for crimes will not by itself resolve the problem of crime, if only because criminals already accept imprisonment as a part of the reality of their lives. It is probably not changes in the "system" but changes in attitudes that move society. System changes are important, but without "consciousness" changes they are often ineffective.

Sugar Bear, as he liked to be called, was one of my best reporters on the male prostitution scene. He'd been hustling since he was about fourteen. He was intelligent, attractive, sexually precocious. His middle-class family, seeing he craved independence and could take care of himself, allowed him to leave home when he wanted to with no hard feelings. He'd been quite successful as a hustler, he reported. Having been "kept" for a while by a well-to-do politician, he'd been introduced to a wealthy clientele. By his mid-twenties, when I met him, he'd traveled extensively and become sophisticated and mature.

With maturation, however, his youthful beauty faded. He was now more manly looking and less marketable, he thought. But he didn't seem to mind; he'd led that life long enough and was happy to stop and take a job as a laborer. It wasn't as glamorous, but it was regular and "honest." He lived in the Tenderloin because he liked the action: for fun, he occasionally still turned tricks. He'd become a sort of protector for new kids on the street. He knew the ropes and was happy to share his knowledge to help newcomers stay out of trouble.

Sugar Bear had two messages to share with the world. The first was that it isn't fair that some people starve while others throw food away. "That's real crime," he said. And the way to make sure that everybody has food is to get them jobs. Everybody has a right to earn a living. The way to solve the problems of prostitution, he told me, is to get everybody to work.

Without jobs kids don't grow up. They never learn responsibility and they never learn self-respect. He was correct about that. The major personality problem I saw among the teenage prostitutes was that they tended to be over-emotional and unrealistic. They still seemed to be playing cops and robbers, only now it was for real. Work certainly might help them grow up, but jobs were hard to come by. I found myself trying to explain to Sugar Bear why unemployment was not so easy to eliminate.

He looked at me incredulously. "Look at all these buildings," he said, pointing around us. "They're wrecks. But they're full of people. Put them all to work cleaning up the city, repairing the buildings. It'd sure be cheaper than putting them all in jail or on welfare."

I started to explain about unions and building regulations, but stopped. I realized I was just buying into the system that in the interests of solving problems, guaranteeing jobs and fair wages, had inadvertently created more problems. Sugar Bear was right.

His second message was that "prostitution is only dirty because society makes it dirty." In America, where prostitution is illicit, it's become part of a criminal scene. Prostitutes he'd met in Europe were professionals, not criminals. They were much better off socially and psychologically. "Prostitution doesn't have to be dirty," he said. "But that means people have to think about it differently."

Toby Marotta loves outrageous proposals as much as I do. One day during a discussion at URSA on the problem of joblessness, he shocked all of us by suggesting that we set up centers to train kids to be vocational prostitutes. There'll be fewer and fewer jobs in the future, he went on to say; automation and inflation are guaranteeing that. People will have more leisure time and will have sex more often. Having sex is a skill. Some people do it well. Those who have the physical resources and the natural inclination and who develop their talents have a right to be paid for their skill, just the way an actor or an athlete is paid. (I was reading James Clavell's *Shogun* at the time. That seemed to be close to how prostitution was viewed in the Japanese culture described in that book. And it was, at least partly, how male prostitution to wealthy women was portrayed in the then-current film *American Gigolo.*)

Toby, of course, didn't think society would embrace his tongue-in-cheek solution for teenage unemployment. But he insisted his prediction of more leisure time and more sex for the affluent was accurate and that, in fact, this would result in an increase in prostitution. He explained, though, that "prostitution" was not a good word for this phenomenon of the near future. Prostitution implies fee schedules, time limits, and exchanges of money. But among the "sexual revolutionaries" that kind of arrangement is rare, he'd found.

More often, he explained, the kids hang around on the streets or in the bars (if they're old enough or can manage to get in), looking for fun, adventure, and sex, hoping for a lucky break, but willing to be satisfied with good sex. When a man comes along who's fat and unattractive—in street jargon, a "troll"—and offers to pay them, if they need the money, they'll go with him and try to get by with as little actual "work" as possible. When a man comes along they find attractive, they may very well approach him; if they like him they'll go with him regardless of the money. (Gay teenagers are pretty aggressive, as most of the adult men we spoke with reported and as we experienced ourselves.) They may mention that they need to buy some clothes or that their rent's due and they may get a hand-out, but that's less important than meeting somebody they like.

That's hardly prostitution in the formal sense. In fact, most of what is called "juvenile prostitution" is just such informal contacts. It is simply the "tricking" of a sexually active life-style with an exchange of money from one person who has to one who has not.

Toby was quite right in saying that what most of the kids want is adult companionship. Cynically they call that finding a "sugar daddy." Behind that cynicism and bravado they put on for one another, most of them, just like most of the rest of us, are hoping to find somebody to love them. For a teenager, alone on the street, living from hand to mouth, the dream of a lover who'll provide a home and some stability is very appealing. The kids who've been on the street too long, of course, may have a hard time settling down and many prospective sugar daddies sour quickly when they see the kids want all the stability with none of the responsibilities. But some men have the patience and understanding to put up with the teenagers' thirst for excitement.

These relationships are heavily stigmatized despite their familiarity in popular mythology (the street boys rescued by generous adult men in Horatio Alger's stories, for instance, or Bruce Wayne and his ward Dick Grayson who fight crime in Gotham City as Batman and Robin). Adults who take kids home risk prison sentences as child molesters. Of course, some may do things to deserve it. But clearly there is a difference that our laws do not recognize between men who court teenage hustlers and those who lurk in bushes to pounce on prepubescent children.

Not all the adults are the patient, well-meaning men I've just described: just as among the general population there are murderers and rapists, so there are among the johns. And certainly the opprobrium heaped upon prostitution tends to scare away well-meaning individuals, leaving a higher percentage of disturbed and criminal men to prey on the hustlers rather than offer them a lucky break.

During the final days of the study, I came to understand the relationships between adults and teenagers in a way even all my interviews with hustlers and johns and experts on prostitution could never have permitted. I'd gone one night to see British filmmaker Graham Coleman's films on Tibetan Buddhism. I was moved and stunned by the final sequence. While Tibetan monks chanted from *The Book of the Dead* a human body was cremated before our eyes. The chants reminded us that life and death are but illusion. All things are but manifestations of our thought forms, impermanent, fading like a mist, bursting like a bubble. Be not afraid, the Tibetan wisdom admonished, look beyond.

I wondered if I shouldn't be looking beyond my experiences in the prostitution study to find the Buddha-truth. I wondered what my thought forms were trying to tell me. After the film and discussion by the filmmaker, I got to talking with a young man who'd been sitting near me. He'd also been moved and stunned. He obviously wanted to talk. We stood on the street for a while and then I invited him over for coffee at the flat nearby where I lived with my three housemates.

I learned he was only eighteen years old. He went by the boyish name Steevy. Having just completed his first year of college at a rather elite and avant-garde school, he was spending the summer in San Francisco with his father. In the fall he was going to the Orient to study for a year. He was quite an accomplished linguist; he'd traveled widely already in Europe and Russia and hoped one day to be an international liaison in either government or industry. He was especially interested in the Orient because it seemed so alien. He was just learning about Buddhism and the religions of the Far East. He was deeply religious, a convert to Russian Orthodoxy, because he loved the chant, the ritual, and the Orthodox mystical tradition. He was fascinated with my knowledge of religion.

Over a period of about six weeks, before I left San Francisco, we got to be friends. Steevy was not a hustler, but from the dynamics of our friendship I came to understand a lot about hustlers and johns.

Even though he lived with a parent, Steevy, like so many of the hustlers, was without friends his own age in the city. With other young people, he said, he felt just as confused as they. With people older he felt more stable and encouraged to grow and expand. He acknowledged freely that he was looking for mature models. He was perhaps unrepresentatively articulate, but I suspect that his attraction to older role models was not that different from that felt by many hustlers and teenagers just discovering confusing sexual (especially homosexual) feelings.

One night I wanted to take Steevy to dinner and a movie that I thought would be thought-provoking for him. I realized I'd have to pay for the evening. Steevy was working as a bicycle messenger for minimum wage and saving everything he made to finance his year in China. He never spent money on luxuries, hardly any on clothes. (I must admit I was sometimes a little embarrassed to be seen with him, because with him in his scruffy shirt and tattered blue jeans I thought we really did look like a hustler and john couple.) I, on the other hand, made fairly good money, was financially secure, and could afford to pay for his dinner. In fact, I would have to if I wanted the evening to come off.

Occasionally he came by during his lunch break. He worked near URSA. When he had no money for lunch I'd give him a couple of dollars. Sometimes he resisted, but most of the time he took it with no hint of embarrassment. Teenagers are used to being paid for by adults; it seems natural to them.

Steevy was an attractive and interesting young man whose company and attentions I enjoyed, but I in no way thought I was exploiting him. He got some free dinners, movies, and a little bit of cash from me, but I didn't think he was exploiting me. The whole notion of exploitation seemed to be meaningless. That is not to say that there is no such thing as out-and-out exploitation or out-and-out prostitution. Of course there are. But the exchange of attention or of money is not itself what makes for exploitation or prostitution.

Perhaps most important of the discoveries inspired by my friendship with Steevy was that the only way one can ever really understand anything is to experience it oneself. That, of course, was what we were trying to approximate through ethnographic observation. But since professional ethics and my own tastes kept me from experiencing the hustler-john relationship directly, I couldn't really understand what such relationships were until I found an analogue in my own life. We can know the truth that others experience only insofar as we are willing to place ourselves in their situations, only insofar as we are compassionate.

Not only is compassion a virtue of the moral life, it is also a category of the epistemological enterprise, I realized. And that was a key to the dilemma I'd been feeling throughout the research. The "truth" I was seeking could only be seen when I would open myself to life, willing to understand others' experience from their perspective.

SEVEN

The Naked Shingles of the World

Old habits must be broken for the hero to see the truth beyond. This does violence both to the perceived world and to the perceiving senses. It demands ordeal: the journey along the road of trials, the three days in the belly of the whale, the meeting with the Lord of the Underworld. To discover the vision of God, the hero must confront suffering and evil.

"I will give you what you desire. I will lead you into solitude. I will lead you by the way you cannot possibly understand, because I want it to be the quickest way," promised (and threatened) the God of Trappist monk and social commentator Thomas Merton.

"To come to the knowledge you have not, you must go by a way in which you know not," declared Spanish mystic John of the Cross.

The hero's journey along a way he knows not may lead him through barren deserts or dark and forboding forests. Monsters lurk in these lonely places at the edge of the world. These monsters are more than simply dangers to be avoided. Like the fish that attacked Tobias, they sometimes have magical properties. They manifest the world-creating powers of the mind, for they define the outer limits of the created world.

The monster in John Gardner's *Grendel,* a retelling of the Beowulf story from the point of view of the monster, is no mindless animal that kills for food or cruel fiend who kills for pleasure (as do demented human beings). He is an intelligent and wise being who understands, or at least struggles to (he is still young), that as a "shadow-shooter, earth-rim-roamer, walker of the world's weird wall" he has a role in the world ecology. Without him in the forest, occasionally snatching up a lost child or devouring an old lady who's wandered too far, the townsfolk would have no way of knowing where the village ended and the forest began. The mind needs boundaries within which to operate. Monsters, embodiments of evil, are the guardians of the boundaries. They patrol "the vast edges drear and naked shingles of the world"; they swim in the menacing coastal waters, instilling pessimistic desolation or fear should one venture too far into the darkness or the depths.

This is primitive evil. This is what children fear in the dark, and what adults cower before when they stand at the edge of a grave and gaze down, fearing that in the place prepared for the steel-vaulted casket of a friend or relative they will see their own face. This is the evil of the impersonal and uncaring universe that heeds no individual rights.

This evil is part of human consciousness. C. G. Jung called the evil and repressed side of the psyche the "shadow." When it isn't allowed into consciousness—through recognition of our own primitive, unruly, destructive, lascivious impulses—it will be projected outward into the world. Jungian analyst and Episcopal priest John A. Sanford writes in *Evil: The Shadow Side of Reality:*

> . . . the human mind is compelled to devise such stories [as the myth of the devil] in order to express and relate to its own archetypal foundations. Today we no longer fashion and follow legends such as this, but the myth-making mind, stripped of its proper function, produces distorted myths. That is, the "devil" is now seen in others, and the mythological picture of God and Satan struggling against each other is projected out into world politics with Russians playing the adversary role for Americans and vice versa. It would be better to have our divine myths back than to fall into the paranoid states of

mind that a mythology projected onto other people produces. (page 116)

The evil lives within us. The demons dance in our dreams. The monsters slither about the foundations of the psyche. Church and state have arisen to patrol the boundaries of the mind. But Church and State have proven to be merely human and venal, easily corrupted, and clutching for authority they do not have. The preachers frighten us with tales of the devil; they are really admonishing us to avoid the unconscious. Politicians rail against human vice and crime; they are really warning us about the dangers of leaving the village.

But beyond the guarded boundaries is the source of life itself. The hero must leave the village and face the monsters head on, for only then can he discover that they are but other manifestations of the Self, and only then can he tame them.

Once I'd moved into the Tenderloin hotel, I let it be known I was interested in talking about prostitution. I said I was writing a book and would pay twenty dollars to hustlers under age eighteen for an interview. A few people looked me up. One of them was a black man named Michael Holmes. He had just gotten out of jail, needed money, and wanted to be interviewed. He said he was seventeen, but since he looked much older I put him off.

He and his friend Eddie, who wore his hair in pickaninny curls like Buckwheat of the Our Gang comedies, worked out with weights in the hall near my room. I'd pass them frequently as I returned in the late afternoon from a day at URSA. I'd usually stop and chat. Michael was still quite insistent that he wanted to make the twenty dollars. One day he described to Toby and me how prostitution worked in prison, how the young and pretty inmates sell sexual favors for protection and commodities. And he told us how he'd been a pimp before going to jail and how he hoped now to reassemble his stable. His girls and two drag queens, he said, were waiting to hear from him.

Well, he was obviously no juvenile. But Toby agreed that he had an interesting story to tell. I decided to fudge the requirements a little and set up the interview.

Michael told me he'd come from a fairly well-off black family in Louisiana. His parents owned a successful restaurant. His brothers and sisters had gone into the business, but he'd never really fit in the family. As early as twelve he'd become sexually active with both girls and boys. He boasted that he was "well hung" (I declined his offer to prove it). He soon learned that white homosexuals would pay for what was for him easy and pleasurable. When his respectable Southern Baptist parents found out, he was told to shape up or get out. Knowing his mother had a soft heart and wasn't really going to disown him and figuring he could survive through his sexual prowess, he decided to leave. He came to San Francisco because his grandmother lived nearby; he'd always been a favorite of hers.

He made quite a hit on the street, developing a regular clientele of men who'd pay as much as seventy-five dollars to fellate him. And he made a hit with the ladies, too, he said. With the money coming in from his own hustling, he could afford to buy the fancy clothes it took to be accepted by the black men he considered peers. Most of them were pimps or players.

"Players," he explained, are "high-class dudes" in urban, black culture. They are not just two-bit pimps, he said. They have real class. He described their culture almost as an atavism of African tribal life. At the center are the players, men who have proven themselves great warriors. Around them gather harems of women and sycophantic men. In exchange for the players' affection they support them in fine style. A successful player has as many as nine or ten followers. For the most part the women work as prostitutes. That is a way to make easy money. It makes their player proud to see his women sexually accomplished and desirable. As they all grow older the women will turn to other jobs, but the relationships will continue. The women raise families. Sometimes they live together, sometimes not. This is a real alternative form of marriage, Michael assured me.

He felt proud being around men like that; he aspired to be one of them. He wanted to be "somebody." But lavishness and style are major criteria for acceptance into the ranks. Players make appearances at certain night clubs, surrounded by their retinues —all dressed to the nines. The attention they get determines acceptance. Looking the part was going to take more money than Michael could make hustling.

A friend soon offered to include him in a heist. They were going after the jewels of a rich black woman who'd shown off her treasures too ostentatiously. She was supposed to be out of town. They got into the house easily enough. It was dark and, not wanting to alarm neighbors who might know she was away, they did not turn on any lights. They were rummaging through the bureau in the bedroom when suddenly, Michael said, there was a noise from the bed. A woman began to scream. They told her to shut up. When she didn't, the friend shot several times. Horrified, Michael turned on the light. He said the bed was just a mass of blood.

They got the jewelry. And Michael made enough money to buy a car and his fancy clothes. But now he was an accessory to murder. He was no street hustler anymore. He was proving himself a warrior. He soon "turned out" several of his lady friends and set out to assemble the full stable that would make him a candidate for player society. Several robberies later, he was again involved in a shooting. This time *he* pulled the trigger, and this time he got caught.

He was sentenced to seven years, of which he served five before being paroled. He'd been a pretty good prisoner, no troublemaker. He got hooked up with a gang of other "high-class dudes" right away and put himself among the upper echelon of inmates: he didn't have to be a troublemaker. The gang called themselves Panthers, he said, though they had no direct connection with the Black Power political group of the '60s. Michael showed me the tattoo of a panther on his forearm that marked him as a member.

He'd got out of prison just a week or two before we met. He said he wanted to go straight. He didn't like stealing or killing. Some of his women were waiting for him because they really loved him and wanted to help him get back on his feet. He still wanted to be a player.

He liked talking to me, he said. He'd never seen a shrink except for diagnostic evaluations in jail. He thought it would be good for him to talk. I declined the official role of therapist, but said I'd be happy to talk anytime he wanted.

Having worked in social services, I was aware how difficult it is for a person who has been institutionalized to ever really develop a normal life. Institutionalization, especially in the penal system, brands one forever. But the difficulties are more immediate than simply stigmatization. The ex-con has a hard time finding a job and is often released from the institution with virtually no means of support.

Michael was trapped in his karma; he could not escape his past. Crime was the only way he knew to make money. His choices, realistically if perhaps fatalistically, were among the kinds of crime. He could live by pimping and hustling, about which he seemed to have certain ethical standards for himself as a "high-class dude," and penny-ante dope dealing, or he could return to stealing and killing. The vice crimes at least seemed to leave open the possibility of some advancement into ordinary society; the crimes of violence closed off all possibilities and simply pushed him back toward prison.

He came by my room a couple of times after that to chat. He wanted me to interview him again for another twenty dollars. I couldn't do that, I said. I didn't like Michael. He seemed just too much a part of the underworld. But I felt an obligation to the research and to my own effort to be unprejudiced and open. I felt a religious obligation to be compassionate and not to write him off as hopeless and beneath me. After all, it was out of such religious motivation that I got myself into this project. I aspired to being what the Buddhists call a bodhisattva, one who through compassion participates in the salvation of the world, helping all beings overcome their karma. I knew it didn't make sense for me to talk in the abstract about saving the juvenile prostitutes when I didn't want to have anything to do with an actual person in that world.

One day Michael came by my room to say that there were some boots on sale at Flagg Brothers that would really suit the outfit he was trying to get together. He only needed twenty-five dollars. He offered me the diamond stud earring he wore as collateral. I lent him the money.

The next time I saw him he said he'd been invited to participate in a robbery, had declined, but didn't see any other way to get any money together. He needed some start-up money before he could bring his women together. He had to buy himself a real outfit, he said. He'd be ashamed for his women to see him looking destitute. Again he asked me for a loan. This time I said no.

Several hours later he came by with a couple of diamond rings. He said he'd give them to me as collateral. In reply to my inquiry, he said he was afraid to pawn them cause one of them was hot and might be identified. Pretty poor collateral, I responded. But he only wanted about a hundred and fifty dollars, he said. The rings were worth over five hundred and if I sold them for cash there'd be no way they could be traced to me. Besides, I'd never have to sell them, he promised.

Okay, I said. And I got him to sign an informal note along with a clear statement that the money was not going to be spent on any criminal activity. The next day I went with him to my bank. He asked me at the last minute to double the amount, arguing that the rings were really valuable. I hesitated, but then capitulated. I found it difficult to say no to him.

Walking back with him from the bank I had the eerie sense that I was never going to see any of the money again. I left Michael and went back to my room. I lay down on the bed atop the faded and tattered spread. I looked around me at that sad little room. The new paint did not hide the chipped and peeling layers from years before. The threadbare carpet and the walls themselves smelled of decay. The mattress sagged beneath me from the weight of too many bodies.

Was I succumbing to the trap of the Tenderloin, I asked myself. Could I end up here not an observer who could go back to a comfortable flat on lovely tree-lined Fair Oaks Street, but a prisoner of the Tenderloin? What was I doing getting involved with Michael Holmes?

I reminded myself that when I was a child my father had been in the business of making loans to poor people to whom banks would not loan. He accepted diamond rings and ramshackle houses as collateral. I suppose, in some ways, that made him a "slum lord," but he was a good man. He never foreclosed on mortgages. He waited patiently and he was usually finally repaid. He was loved by many people among San Antonio's poor because he'd trusted them and given them the chance to improve their lives. I wondered what he'd have thought of my connection with Michael. I wondered if he'd ever been in a similar situation.

Street noise percolated up through the buzz of traffic, a background for my troubled ruminations. Occasionally a shouted obscenity or the loud honking of a horn broke through the hubbub and caught my attention. Suddenly, clearly, from a radio somewhere came a melody I recognized: George Harrison singing "My Sweet Lord." The song had long signified for me my desire to see God. Now it reminded me of my commitment to find that vision in my everyday experience. Wasn't this sleazy hotel room and my curious involvement with Michael just as truly an experience of God?

I told myself I had to trust Michael. After all, I wanted to live in a universe of trust. I made sure people could trust me; the only way I could trust others was just to do it. After all, trust doesn't mean certainty. The whole point of trust is that one is taking a risk.

Besides, I reminded myself, twice before I'd been robbed; each time had taught me a lesson and resulted in a breakthrough in my life. The first time was after I'd virtually fled San Francisco when the first real love affair of my life soured after my beloved took up with one of my housemates. I'd gone to the Midwest to visit friends and to attend the wedding of my steady girlfriend in college. Hitchhiking back from Chicago, I'd had my backpack and sleeping bag stolen. One of the few things I had left was a book of Buddhist texts from which I'd been reading the bodhisattva's vow to accept the suffering of the world out of compassion for other suffering beings. Once I got over the shock of the robbery, I found all my lovesickness, jealousy, and possessiveness gone along with the pack. The second time, I'd had my journal stolen along with some other things I'd left on the seat of a car. I was terribly upset, but out of it I resolved my dilemma about finishing graduate school, and I started my career in mental health.

I was now in my mid-thirties. I was expecting the predictable mid-life crisis. Maybe I was in it. I wasn't sure what I was doing studying prostitution. I was following Toby, the Guardian Angel, but I was feeling we'd gone off in a strange direction. I was feeling rootless and despondent. Perhaps I had another lesson to learn—one that had to do with trust. Perhaps Michael was an instrument of divine intervention, I thought. Even if I lost the money, the lesson would be worth it. I wasn't sure I could trust Michael Holmes, but I decided I'd trust God.

The next time I saw Michael he was very pleased with his progress. He said he was going to an event at one of the players' clubs and had put together quite an outfit. He asked me if I

wanted to go along, as one of his "boys." I declined the invita-
tion. I was already beginning to feel strangely powerless around
Michael. I didn't want to further that by slipping into one of the
roles in his culture. Besides, I wasn't one of his "boys."

He then showed me a hand gun he'd just acquired, a necessary part of his costume, he explained. I asked him to put it
away. He insisted on playing with it a while before returning it
to its place in his dresser. Again he wanted to borrow some
money. He offered the gun as collateral. I said I didn't want
anything to do with the gun. He didn't get any more money
from me that night. But, as he must have known, the gun had
frightened me.

I was actually getting a good deal of information from Michael. He told me about his and others' experiences in the prostitution trade. He explained things I would not have
understood or seen otherwise. I felt this justified my having
gotten so involved with him: I was supposed to be doing research. But I felt tainted by the involvement. I felt I couldn't
share with Toby or, especially, my supervisor at URSA the
connection I'd developed. While Michael assured me the
money I'd lent him wasn't going to set up his pimping business,
I suspected it probably was. I feared that even the suggestion
that I'd been financing a prostitution ring could be used to in-
validate the whole study. On the other hand, I thought my
managing to gather information through such an inside source
might make the study a greater success. It seemed the ethnographic approach required risk.

I'd occasionally ask Michael about the money he owed me.
He'd acknowledge the debt, ask for a little more time, assuring
me that things were just about to take off. He'd sometimes hint
that if I had to have the money he'd get it, implying that he could
steal it. That always forced me to reiterate that my reason for
lending him the money was to keep him from going back to the
life of crime, that the money really didn't matter that much.

Usually he'd then ask for more. Sometimes I'd give it to him, wondering what I was doing.

Michael was beginning to scare me. I felt I was losing control over myself; I was feeling confused. I did not understand what this was all about. But I did understand that the hero's path is called the Road of Trials.

One day I went to see Michael Holmes just after seeing Reverend Jane Spahr, my spiritual director. (Without her help I'd never have made it through this whole experience!) We had come to talk about Michael as a vampire. Of course he wasn't one of the "living dead," but he had a curious power over me that seemed like that attributed to the Draculas and Nosferatus of popular myth. I'd made an agreement with Janie that morning to confront Michael on his vampirism and certainly not to give him any more money.

Michael was very stoned when I arrived. He began by saying that he needed a thousand dollars as good faith money in a deal to establish his bordello in a motel in Sacramento. I said no. I certainly wasn't going to pay for a bordello. But more important, I'd made an agreement.

Michael got quite agitated. (It was almost as though I'd held a crucifix in the vampire's face.) He started dancing around the room, talking about how important this was and how this would be the last loan because it would give him the income to pay me back twofold.

I'd said I didn't want back more than he'd actually borrowed and that I'd be patient. I wasn't going to give him any more. I had an agreement with Janie. I reminded him that he had an agreement with me. Agreements are sacred.

Michael challenged my commitment to the agreement. He got out his gun and asked if that would convince me to violate the agreement. I said no. He was pointing the gun at my face, jeering at me. He seemed so drugged that I wasn't sure his behavior was predictable. I was terrified. I certainly didn't think my life was worth the money. He could have it. But I had made an agreement.

I felt I was being tested by the universe. In fact, the whole relationship with Michael seemed some kind of test of faith. I wasn't quite sure what I was expected to do, but I knew I couldn't avoid the test—at least not then with a gun aimed at me.

I remained firm. After a while Michael calmed down and apologized. He assured me he was just joking. I told him I didn't like that kind of joke and reminded him that I had gotten involved with him in the first place out of spiritual motives. I was hoping that my "grace," won through the effort to be trusting and nonpossessive, could conquer his "karma." I was not interested in making money, but in "saving" him. He seemed to understand that a little.

The next time I saw him he described a near "mystical" experience. He said he'd been half awakened from sleep by an angel standing over his bed telling him that if he didn't put his life in order he'd die very young, and that he was being given a chance to change. He said he knew I was that chance. And he said that later that day he'd given the last dollar or two in his pocket to a destitute old woman, recognizing that his own generosity was being tested. These testimonies of righteousness seemed a little out of character, but I was willing to believe my grace was actually transforming him. (And maybe it was.)

Soon, at the insistence of his parole officer, Michael got a job as a short-order cook at a Sambo's. He stopped asking for money, but still wanted to see me. He said one day that he was in love with me and wanted me to be his lover. I was shocked. I told him I had no interest in him sexually or emotionally. We had a business deal; I wanted to help him get back on his feet; I understood how difficult it can be for an ex-convict to break the criminal cycle, but that was all. He seemed a little rejected, but insisted that he'd show me what a "sharp nigger" he really was and that he'd always be my friend.

Then suddenly one day Michael disappeared. I heard nothing from him. He'd checked out of his hotel. After a couple of weeks I took the rings he'd given me as collateral to a jeweler. They were fakes. I figured the money was gone. I regretted losing it, but I was relieved that Michael too was gone.

EIGHT

The Lord
of the Underworld

Death is Lord of the Underworld. The hero must face his own dissolution in order to see that his true identity is not his ego; it is not clear to him, of course, what else there is of him besides ego. Death frightens us all. We can only hope to recall some hint of the age-old wisdom when the Lord of the Underworld tests us. We pass the test only if we can manage to say, "I am not afraid."

I'd finished my stint in the Tenderloin and was waiting for federal clearance to start the visits to other cities. On that first round I'd be going to New York and Boston with Toby and briefly to Houston by myself. One day several months after his disappearance Michael Holmes called me. He was in Louisiana. He was returning to San Francisco and he wanted to see me. I said I really didn't want to see him again. He insisted, almost pleading, saying he'd explain everything.

A week later I met him in his hotel room. He said he had to tell me the truth. He hadn't been successful in establishing his pimping business because as soon as he'd been noticed he was approached by members of the Panthers. He was told that the protection he'd gotten in prison wasn't free. He was expected to work for them on the outside.

They'd been waiting for him to show up at the headquarters for assignment, they said. Then they roughed him up some and warned that next time he wouldn't survive their visit. When he went for an assignment, he was told to "hit" two guys in Oakland who'd been cheating the organization's drug-dealing network.

That was where his gun had come from, he explained. They'd supplied the weapon.

He said he'd killed a number of people for them, then got scared and had run back home to Louisiana. Just shortly before he called me, they'd contacted him there and reminded him he had an assignment waiting and that it wasn't so easy to leave the organization. So he'd returned to find out what it would take to leave. He could buy his "contract," he said, for five thousand dollars. His grandmother had put up most of the money, but he still needed more. Could I help?

I felt in an awful bind. I didn't want to give him more money. But I also didn't want to see him get killed. And I didn't want to see him killing anybody else. I'd called myself a pacifist during the Vietnam War. Now maybe I had to act on those beliefs. Could I morally justify keeping money sitting in the bank while Michael was killing people? On the one hand, of course, it was none of my business. On the other, I realized, I was responsible for everything that happened in my universe.

In religious life I had learned to live simply. I made more money than I spent. I was saving so I could retire to be a hermit of some sort. I enjoyed the thought of the money in the bank. But wasn't letting that money accumulate really just being a miser?

So far, apparently, Michael had only been asked to hit other members of the gang, I rationalized. But it was still murder. And even if the story were a lie, how could I morally put my pleasure in accumulating money before his sin of killing? I worried about it for a long time, but it seemed as if there was only one way to pass this test.

I agreed to help him.

Not long after that Michael called me at URSA, saying he had to talk with me. We met in a park downtown. He seemed very anxious. He said he knew he wasn't repaying the loan, that he'd told me too much about himself, and that he feared I'd go to his parole officer and he'd end up back in prison. He'd lain awake all night, he said, thinking that he just ought to kill me, then he'd have nothing to fear.

O God, I thought, what have I gotten myself into? One day he loves me. The next he is going to kill me. I assured him I wasn't going to go to the police. I had no desire to see him in jail again. I certainly wouldn't get my money back then. He accepted that. He seemed relieved, but added that just for his protection he'd told one of his cronies about me and had instructed the friend to come after me if he were arrested.

Death seemed closer to me than it ever had before.

Then it was fall. Toby and I left for Boston and New York. We lived in a hotel just off Times Square. From that perspective, New York is a very ugly city. Still, it had been good not having Michael after me. We were away about two months. A week or two after my return, Michael called. He said he'd been working and would soon have some money to give me. He thanked me profusely for being patient and said he was glad I was home. He'd missed me. I put off seeing him, though I did meet him for breakfast finally. He paid for it. Things seemed peaceful. The confrontation with Death seemed to have been avoided. I was relieved.

The peace lasted less than a month. It was broken early one Saturday morning—not by Michael, but by Bob Benedict, a client I'd seen at the Tenderloin Clinic a couple of years before. He lived in the Tenderloin and I'd run into him recently. He called me about two A.M. to beg for help.

About a week before he'd told me proudly that a prostitute who hadn't wanted her baby had given him the child to take care of. That had meant a lot to him. Shortly before I'd seen him at the Clinic he'd lost custody of his own child in a divorce. Because he'd been hospitalized for a psychiatric disorder, his wife maintained he was an unfit parent and should have no parental rights to their daughter. This had been particularly traumatic for him. When he was a boy he'd been left to baby-sit his infant sister. The baby died, apparently of unexplained crib death. Of course, his parents blamed him. That had been the start of his psychiatric problems. Losing rights to see his own child brought up again all the guilt and fear that had surrounded his sister's death.

He was still fighting for some custody of the child. Taking care of the prostitute's baby seemed a chance to prove he could be a fit parent. But apparently early that Saturday morning his dream had turned into a nightmare.

Something was wrong with the baby, he told me. I advised him to go to a hospital. He was afraid to do that; the court would find out, and he'd lose his child forever. I talked with him a while, really just trying to get him to take care of the matter on his own. It was the middle of the night. I just did not want to get involved beyond giving some advice on the phone.

Quite recently I'd seen the movie *Ordinary People*. The memory of the psychiatrist's going down to meet his suicidal client in the middle of the night came back to me. They might do that in movies, I'd thought, but in reality that's considered bad practice. But in the movie it had saved a life. Now Bob was begging me to save the baby and save him. I tried to put him off. Almost everything can wait till morning, I assured. But then, beginning to scream, he said the baby was turning blue.

I woke Leslie to explain what had happened and to borrow her car. As fast as I could I drove down into the Tenderloin and found the address. Bob was waiting outside crying. We went up to his room. The place was a shambles. But there was no baby. Bob was hysterical; he could barely talk. He just kept saying, "She's not here, she's not here."

I got him calmed down and he said he'd start at the beginning. His story moved quickly through how delighted he'd been with the baby, but then how helpless he'd felt when it cried. He wanted it to love him, but it was only concerned with its own wants. He'd grown depressed and then angry.

He started sobbing and screaming. He then calmed down enough to say he'd wrapped the baby in a brown paper bag and buried it in Golden Gate Park the day before. "What can I do now?" he begged me. He was afraid of going to the police because he'd once been brutally beaten by a policeman.

I was stunned by that revelation. This was much more serious than I'd expected. I told him he could go to the psychiatric hospital. He agreed, saying he wanted to be locked up. I told him to get his things together and we'd go right away. He seemed dazed but obeyed me. He got some clothes out of a drawer and then went into the bathroom.

He came out with a sort of ornamental dagger. "Look here," he said, sticking the point into the wall. "This is how the cuts were in the baby—this same shape, only they were full of blood."

"Come on, Bob, let's go."

"No," he screamed. I wondered when the building manager was going to come to the door to tell us to cut out the racket. "I don't want to go to the hospital. I'll kill myself. I can jump out the window." It was a five-floor drop to a concrete slab.

"Bob, you don't have to die. We can go to the hospital and they'll help you." I had talked him out of suicide several times before.

"You don't care about me," he suddenly shouted at me wildly. "You just want to take me there so you can watch them kill me. This whole thing was your idea. I know that. You made me kill the baby and now you want me to kill myself so you can write a book about it."

He started jabbing at me with the dagger. I grabbed hold of his wrists and held him. He was strong but I thought if I could just hold him a while without getting into a real fight he'd calm down.

Now he was sobbing softly, talking about the voices in his head: his father, blaming him for the baby's death, calling him a shit over and over. He still clutched the dagger tight. He looked over at a paper bag lying half open on the floor and startled, saying he could see the baby all cut up in the bag.

Every so often he'd get angry with me again, but most of the time he just cried or listened to the voices. But whenever I'd relax my grip, he'd start to thrash about and lunge at me. He was between me and the door. I knew I couldn't make it past him safely. The dagger wasn't that sharp, but in the back it could easily kill me.

I fought to keep down my own fear. I remembered the advice of the Tibetan Book of the Dead. It was all a dream, a deadly dream, but nothing to be afraid of. I was only fearful for my ego. That was all I could lose. And that wasn't worth much in the long run anyway.

And I remembered that I was, after all, Bob's therapist. That gave me some kind of power over him. If I stayed calm and showed that I believed he could pull himself together, he probably would. I kept up a slow patter of talk, urging him to stay in control. He told me how much he loved me, but how frightened he was.

We both fell silent for a while. He looked off into space to his left, listening to the voices, then grew very calm. He looked at me straight in the eye and said matter-of-factly, "There's nothing we can do. Let's just get this over with."

I felt a scream in my throat and heard a voice inside my own head begging him not to kill me. Not here. Not now. But I kept it inside. Dying like this in a sleazy Tenderloin hotel didn't fit any of my expectations, but, I told myself, it was okay. I'd done what had seemed like the compassionate act in coming here. I did not want to spoil my death by regretting anything as insignificant as the circumstances.

For a moment I looked beyond the boundaries. For a moment I knew I could accept death; I didn't have to be afraid. And at the same time, I knew I didn't have to die. Bob started to pull away to get some leverage with the knife. I held his wrist tighter.

"No, Bob," I stated, firmly. "Give me the knife," I ordered. He looked dazed. I released the other wrist and took the knife from his hand. Only then did I begin to tremble. Before I was overwhelmed and while I still had command, I ordered him to get the things on the bed and come with me.

He followed obediently and I drove him to Mount Zion Hospital where I knew friends of mine would be on duty. Once there, Bob started fighting again. This time it took four security guards to subdue him and put him in restraints. He wouldn't talk to the doctor beyond shouting obscenities. He was given an injection of an antipsychotic drug and fell asleep. I went home.

In the morning I called the psych facility. I was told that after the drug had worn off, he'd seemed clear. He denied the story about the baby and said he really wouldn't have hurt me. They released him.

After a couple of days I'd calmed down. Bob called me about that time and apologized. He said he just didn't know what had come over him. He said he thought the story about the baby had been a bad dream. I had the feeling my whole life was turning into a bad dream.

Early the next week Michael Holmes called me at work to say he'd come by my house with seventeen hundred dollars in cash to give me, but nobody was there. I thanked him and instructed him to put it in an envelope addressed to me and put it through the mail slot.

A few hours later, as I was preparing to leave work, Michael showed up at URSA. He said he'd left all the money he had at my house and wanted to borrow twenty-five bucks. I said no, that didn't make any sense. When he persisted, I agreed to go home with him to my house and give him some money out of what he'd left. He agreed. In fact, he was with a friend who had a car and who offered to drive us there.

There was no envelope. Michael insisted he'd left it. We hunted around in case one of my housemates had picked up the mail, but no it wasn't there. I told Michael I just didn't believe him. He got quite angry, said I was calling him a liar and challenging his manhood. He threatened me. He said the only thing that would appease him would be for me to return the seventeen hundred as a sign of my faith in him.

"What seventeen hundred dollars?" I said incredulously.

He called me later that night to reiterate a vague but fatal-sounding threat. And then called me at URSA in the morning. I was polite. I thanked him for his effort, said I didn't know what happened to the money. It was okay, just don't call any more. And I hung up before he had a chance to say anything.

That weekend I went to Yosemite with friends. I wanted to get away from the city and to find silence and the chance to be with God in the open mountains. I feared I might not get another such chance in this life.

Monday, accompanied by another man, Michael's friend with the car showed up at the apartment with another envelope. My housemate Gary was home. They asked for a receipt this time. Gary went to get a pen. The men followed him into the flat, pulled a knife on him, tied him up with wire from the stereo, and rummaged through the house. They demanded to know where the jewels and the cocaine were—Michael must have had an inflated notion of my worth! They took a camera and typewriter of mine, my Phi Beta Kappa key, the cash in the kitchen we pitched in for the week's food, and Gary's camera. They messed up Ernst's room and Leslie's room, but found nothing to steal.

Once they were gone Gary got out of the wire bonds pretty easily and called me. We went to the police. They were singularly unhelpful, accusing me of protecting Michael because I did not want to give his name to the cop at the station until I'd explained the threat he'd made on my life. I honestly feared that police would go question him and, to protect himself against my testimony, he'd go ahead and "hit" me as he had others before. I insisted on waiting till I could speak with a police detective.

I found myself quite anxious after we got home. I feared

walking down the block from the bus stop, answering the door-bell, and standing near a window. After a day or two I pulled myself together and realized if I handled the fear of death two weeks before with Bob Benedict, I could do it again. And I could take sensible precautions to protect myself. The police advised me to buy a gun and "blow him away" if Michael came to the door. I didn't think that very sensible advice. (I couldn't see myself answering the door with a pistol in my hand.) I resigned myself mentally and spiritually to accept whatever future awaited me. And I arranged to move out of the flat.

By this time everybody at URSA knew the story. They were all sympathetic and supportive. I was invited to move in with Sally Jones, one of the other URSA personnel. My calls were screened by the telephone operator: when Michael called he was told I'd left town.

The next Sunday I was sitting in a church pew, nervously beg-ging God for understanding and for help. Only a few weeks before I'd been sitting happily in my kitchen talking with Leslie and Robin. I'd felt perplexed by some of my experiences. But I'd felt blessed. I figured I'd passed the test with Michael. He had a job; all I had to do was wait and I'd see the fruits of my generosity. I'd thought my hero's journey was over and all that was left for me was to develop some sort of philosophical recon-ciliation between sex and spirituality, pretty much along the lines of Robin's description of her life.

But then within those few weeks my life had fallen apart. My efforts to see good in the sexual underworld had come to nothing. I'd nearly been stabbed to death in a sleazy hotel room. I'd been tricked out of my savings. My apartment had been burglarized. My life was threatened. I'd fled my home and was "in hiding" at Sally's.

The night Bob Benedict had called me, as I was getting into bed, I heard on the radio the New Wave rock group Blondie singing their new song, "The Tide is High." That metaphor had become particularly appropriate. I felt I was doing my best to keep from being swept away by a tide of misfortune and danger.

I'd come to church partly out of routine. I wasn't sure I wanted to sing happy hymns and listen to a sermon on how sweet Jesus can be. But I'd come anyway. I was committed to my belief that religious practice can spark insight and I needed some insight. Besides, I was just a little superstitiously afraid God might wash more misfortune over me if I didn't.

I sat in the back of the church, more caught up in my anxiety than in real prayer, beseeching heaven for help. I didn't believe in the puppet master God who solves problems if asked politely enough. I told myself I believed in a more sophisticated spirituality that recognized the divine as a manifestation of my deepest thought forms. But that Sunday, I'd have settled for any help I could get.

With little enthusiasm, I followed the words in the hymnal of the opening song and paid scant attention to the announcements and the exhortations to rejoice in the Lord. After the choir had sung something I didn't really hear, I sat back to fret during what I expected to be a mindless sermon that could say nothing to me about the bizarre condition my life was suddenly in.

"The mother eagle builds its nest with thorns and briars," the preacher began, explaining an ancient Hebrew bestiary. "She covers these with mud and then cushions the interior with soft feathers. She lays her eggs and lovingly watches over them till they hatch. As long as the eaglets are small, the eagle feeds them and keeps the aerie clean, warm, and soft for them. But when they're old enough to fly she begins to dismantle the nest, pulling out first the soft feathers and then the mud, leaving only the briars and thorns."

The preacher was tall. Both his beard and hair were well trimmed and close-cropped. His blue eyes flashed with excitement and a sometimes childlike defiant glee. His preaching voice carried a drawl and cadence that revealed his background as a Southern Baptist. He'd come to California, I knew, several years before, developed a more sophisticated theology, and took over pastorship of an avant-garde metropolitan church.

"The mother eagle destroys the nest to force her young to grow up and fly out on their own," the preacher explained. "God sometimes drives us out of our complacency, makes us grow up and fly, by plucking away the feathers and mud that have made our lives soft and cushy, to get us off our ass and get us on with our lives."

It was the First Sunday of Advent, according to ancient tradition a time to prepare for the coming of the Christ consciousness, ritually celebrated each year at the time of the winter solstice when the sun is reborn out of the darkness of the year's end. For primitive people each year there had been a gnawing anxiety that last year's sins had been too grievous, that the gods would not smile, that the descent of the sun toward the horizon would not reverse. Then the days would dwindle and the nights prolong until the light was eaten up. Years of experience and scientific observation have confirmed the pattern of eternal return. But modern humankind still fears the unknown future. Financial insecurity, pre-Christmas anxiety, and depression are modern variants of the age-old fear of darkness still ritualized in Advent.

This was an occasion, I understood from the sermon, to realize our fears and discomforts and pledge ourselves to go on, to learn how to fly. That Advent it was easy for me to realize my discomforts. In the past months the soft feathers had been plucked from my comfortable nest, and, then in the last two weeks, the mud. Now only the briars remained. But I hadn't known how to fly. I hadn't understood what all this misfortune had meant.

Suddenly according to that image of the Advent eagle, I understood these experiences as part of my spiritual life. Of course, years before I'd read Joseph Campbell's *The Hero with a Thousand Faces.* I'd thought of life as a puzzle and the hero journey as a major clue to piecing it all together. But though I had occasionally thought about the prostitution study in terms of that myth pattern, it was not until that moment that all the pieces fell into place.

As the service continued, I felt the burden of worry lift. I saw that Michael and Bob were the monsters of the Underworld, that I'd confronted them and was now being given the last bit of help I needed to pass the test. God was answering my prayer. The insight was there: the power Michael had over me was in my own mind. As the Tibetan Book of the Dead had said, and as I'd recalled the night with Bob in the Tenderloin, all that threatens is but a manifestation of our own thought forms.

I realized that the passage through the Underworld was complete. It was time for what Campbell called "the magic flight." It was time for me to leave San Francisco and begin a new phase of adventure. And I realized the boon I was to bring back with me.

My problems were not solved. The money was still gone and the threat was still hanging over my head. But somehow it all made sense.

I had lent the money to Michael in the first place to "save" him, to see if the universe could be trusted, to see if by trusting the universe I could create for myself a trustable universe. It appeared I'd been unsuccessful. Michael wasn't trustworthy. The universe didn't seem to reflect my innocence. What was I to learn from that experience?

I got involved with Michael only because I'd found myself in the Tenderloin, amidst people whose universe and values were radically different from mine. In the traditional world, bound by class and racial lines, I'd never have met a man like Michael Holmes. But in the modern world, we are all exposed to a multitude of such people. That is what Michael represented in my life: the defenselessness we all experience before the modern world.

No matter who one is or how one lives, today it is almost impossible to cloister oneself. Even the very rich, if they go outside their mansions, are exposed to the variety of pluralistic

America. Struggle between classes, races, ethnic groups, and special interest groups characterizes modern life.

For me, Michael Holmes was a personification of the continuing struggle and effort that modern life demands. I made a choice —as I see it, the only one I could—to be humane and compassionate. I chose to champion human values even in the face of inhumanity. On the one hand, of course, I got burned. I didn't have my trust validated. Yet, wouldn't it have been unrealistic if I had?

The message of our conflict with the modern world is not that the problems will be solved, but that we must learn to live with them without destroying our humanity. If people avoid the problems, becoming aloof and cold, not wanting to be bothered by other people's hurts because they might get hurt themselves, the problems will only get worse.

The problems of the sexual underworld, for instance, will not be solved by laws aimed at "protecting the family" or by restricting all sex-linked businesses to the sex-trade zones. Such efforts, though seemingly effective in the short run, will only exacerbate the problems in the long run.

The fact is we have to face the problems and we have to maintain our innocence even then. I could have avoided the problems with Michael Holmes or Bob Benedict had I, at the beginning, said "I don't want to get involved." But I'd have closed myself off. I might have avoided the traumatic experiences and saved some money, but my life would have been poorer. I wouldn't have done battle with the monsters and I wouldn't have won any wisdom. No one becomes a hero by avoiding risks.

I'd never have learned to recognize the shadow in myself if I hadn't seen it projected outside. Michael was my shadow: in dealing with him I was dealing with a part of myself. In recognizing his unworthiness I had to recognize my own. I had to take responsibility for my own tendency to be inhumane, to exploit the world, to cheat, to get something for nothing.

In the sense that Michael represented the modern world, his

lack of trustworthiness represented the lack of faith in the world we all feel. We are without faith; we do not trust our lives. The old myths do not satisfy us. In a strange way, I got something to believe in from Michael. I saw the pattern of the hero in my struggle with him.

I was asked once what I'd do if I had to choose between being a rich man living in Manhattan, amidst modern technology and luxury, having the money to buy pleasure and attention, but feeling alienated from nature and from people around me, or being a peasant living in Haiti, amidst squalor, eking out a poor existence, but feeling connected with all my tribe and, through primitive religion, with all the nature spirits. I answered that I saw no real choice at all. Of course, I'd choose to be the Haitian. The sense of meaning is all that really counts in life. Everything else is "dust in the wind."

But I am neither of those. I am, I suppose, somewhere in the middle—where most of us find ourselves. And so, amidst the technology and luxury and alienation and hassle of modern life, we must seek meaning. That meaning makes us rich. I'd lost a lot of money, but I soon realized a sort of promise from God that no matter how meager my income, I'd always be able to live more simply and more cheaply, so long as I was motivated by my sense of meaning. That actually guarantees all the riches I could need.

After a week or two I got an appointment with a detective in the central police department. He traced Michael Holmes' record and found he'd been arrested for street fighting a couple of times. That was all. He'd never been in prison and had probably never murdered anybody. Since we couldn't identify the men who'd actually done the robbery, the police didn't pursue the case any further. I was relieved to realize the threats were probably vain. And now that I'd gone to the police, Michael really couldn't risk killing me.

I stayed in hiding through December, then went on a sailing

cruise in the Caribbean I'd scheduled six months earlier, thinking the study would be over by then. That was the first real vacation of my life, and I needed it. After making the commitment to follow the clues and leave San Francisco as soon as the study was complete, things changed.

The Sufi Teacher in Reshad Feild's *The Last Barrier* explains:

> . . . the rose bush can produce a perfect rose only through correct pruning. The pruning may hurt the plant temporarily, but if the plant were able to understand the necessity, then it would be filled with joy each time the gardener came with the knife. (page 60)

I'd survived. I'd faced death. I'd done battle with a vampire. I'd been guilty of hubris, I realized, in thinking my "grace" could conquer his "karma": when one meets a vampire, one should steer clear. But I'd had my adventure on the Road of Trials. I'd crossed the boundaries and seen a world beyond my normal experience. I'd managed to remind myself that the monsters, however truly life-threatening, were but manifestations of my own thought forms. I'd glimpsed the background behind my experience. I'd found the message in that sermon of the First Sunday of Advent.

And I'd come back from my adventure bearing boons. I'd seen what could make our sexual revolution responsible. I'd seen how to transform vision.

And I'd remembered the wisdom. The briars and thorns in the now dismantled nest of my life in San Francisco and in the briar patch of the Tenderloin were not to harm, but to save, to blossom with roses, to hint at the hidden reality—we call it God—that works to transform our vision and to bring us all to Resurrection, here and now.

PART II

American Bodhisattva

From your spirit where can I flee?
If I go up to the heavens, you are there;
if I sink to the underworld, you are present there.
If I take the wings of the dawn,
if I settle at the farthest limits of the sea,
even there your hand is ever upon me,
you lead me and hold me fast.

PSALM 139

NINE

The Many Realities

Throughout history, religion has helped us deal with dramatic social change. Prophets, messiahs, and charismatic leaders have appeared at critical times. These religious figures have both reacted to and facilitated attitudinal changes that pushed society through the crises. Not all these resolutions to crises have been progressive. Recently many figures have appeared establishing cults that promise some escape from the tumult of modern life. The leaders of the Christian Right who have achieved prominence in the early 1980s are such figures.

We are at a critical time in the history of consciousness. The science and technology upon which our culture is based have undone the belief structures of the past. Naive and fundamentalist interpretations of our religions no longer make sense. We are rightfully confused and even resentful.

Even as the old realities have been undone, new ones have arisen that challenge our understanding of life even further. We have begun to see ourselves as but specks within a universe in which the basic unit is not the nation nor even the planet nor planetary system, but the galaxy. Only very recently we have achieved a vantage point beyond the planetary surface. We are just beginning to develop a cohesive consciousness of ourselves as a collective planetary being. We are understandably caught in an "identity crisis."

In *The Myth of the Great Secret* I described this contemporary identity crisis as an "epistemological malaise": we do not know what is true. In fact, this identity crisis manifests the age-old conundrum of the mythical and mystical traditions. We don't know what consciousness is. We don't know who we are. What and who we really are is a Great Secret.

Some people today are turning back to the religions of their childhoods, preferring to avoid facing the contradictions between these faiths and modern realities. Seeing that the world is becoming too threatening, they seek to return to what they recall as the simplicity of the past. These feelings are understandable, but the example, for instance, of the fundamentalist theocratic state that arose in Iran in the late '70s should warn us of what a return to orthodoxy can cost in lives and freedom.

For others the only intelligent—though not particularly comforting—response to the modern religious dilemma is agnostic skepticism. They have given up belief in supernatural fantasies and accepted the hard realities of the material world. But in adjusting their world view to modern scientific fact, they have impoverished their experience of life. Meaning and direction have been lost.

Paradoxically, though this skepticism has been damaging to the Churches, it parallels a familiar stage in the development of the individual spiritual life. According to great mystics and religious visionaries of the past, the realization of the emptiness of religious truth is frequently a necessary step in the growth of the spirit. For conventional belief is merely an attachment of ego. As philosopher of religion Wilfred Cantwell Smith observes, the end of religion (in the sense of aim or goal) is the end of religion (in the sense of termination)—that is, the transcendence of doctrinaire beliefs.

The image of the hero's journey seems particularly appropriate for us today. That journey is the quest to discover the hero's deepest identity. We have, like it or not, been thrown out of the village. As a people we stand at the first threshold. It is very dark. Before us, in the guise of nuclear war, urban crime, the new sexuality, and all the rest, loom the monsters of the Underworld. The voices calling us to return to the village, warning us of sin and damnation if we venture further, tempt us to abandon the journey.

But it is only by continuing the journey that we can hope to be saved. Then what seems the contemporary demise of religion, its death throes visible perhaps in the resurgence of anachronistic fundamentalism, can be the occasion for the birth of a modern spiritual consciousness, which is a realization of our individual and collective identity.

This consciousness recognizes that we have erred in reducing reality to simple historical and statistical factuality. For there are also symbolical, mythical, and metaphorical realities. Indeed, because these are often much closer to us than historical events, they may be said to possess "more" reality. Myth, the accumulation of revered belief, may be said to be more real than history, for what people *think* happened in the past affects them in the present much more than what "actually" happened.

In a very real way religion has aimed at saving the world. We can only save the modern world by developing a religious consciousness that is equal to it, that is willing to engage it and to solve its problems from within. The spiritual teachings no longer have to—or can—carry the burden of explaining the physical world. As the myths make sense to us today with our modern perspective and sophistication, they reveal how much bigger life is than we ordinarily perceive, and ourselves how much more than just individualized egos clashing into one another. Such a view of religion shifts our epistemological assumptions. We can solve our identity crisis by changing our fundamental notions of truth: we see that the way things really are is totally different from what we usually think. And we can save religious consciousness by understanding religion as a source not of fact or correct opinion, but of meaning.

I found meaning in my experience in the Tenderloin by understanding it in terms of the hero myth. Such "mythologizing" of our lives, finding in them echoes of themes that convey meaning, transforms vision by allowing the other realities to penetrate the everyday reality, reminding us of our deepest identity (which is as the hero of myth and religion). Thus, while maintaining our intelligence and modernity, we can find the richness of meaning that our ancestors perceived in the world around them. Moreover, to their perceptions of the levels of being, we can add our own technological and scientific perceptions. For modern consciousness, seeming, on the one hand, to reduce the world to purely mechanistic processes, is, on the other, re-articulating the levels of reality according to the languages of physics and psychology.

Spiritual consciousness recognizes that our true identity is rooted deeply in a "transpersonal" reality. Our modern hero quest must be to find that transpersonal reality and express it in ways that make sense today. It is the consciousness of these roots that should be the basis for developing guidelines for behavior.

Critics of modern sexuality seem correct in bemoaning the contemporary lack of norms. Too many people, in the name of "liberating" themselves, end up imprisoning themselves in a new set of sexual neuroses. They feel bored, lonely, and jaded, unable to tolerate intimacy or to find meaning for their lives. But meaningful norms for behavior cannot be imposed from the past. To find guidelines for our sexual revolution, we must look to our experience of consciousness. The virtues that grace a life, while they stand on their own as worthwhile qualities, are more compelling if they are founded in a religious/mystical vision. That is what theology is really supposed to provide. And that is what my experiences in the prostitution study forced me to find.

My novicemaster during my first year as a Catholic religious, Father Herbert Pieper, once rebuked me for believing in mystical pretensions. He'd taken my mystical language, he said, simply as an undisciplined literary device. He was more right than I think he knew.

Father Pieper was one of the few truly holy men I've known. He taught me and my fellow novices to take responsibility for our religious observance and not to rely on obedience to rules. He taught us to look beyond the rules to what they intended, which was, in essence, that we grow intellectually, emotionally, and spiritually. And he taught us to understand the doctrines of religion in the same way.

Father Pieper exposed the class of novices, young men fresh out of high school, to the most sophisticated contemporary analyses of the Christian Scriptures. He taught us that revelation was expressed in the linguistic styles of the various phases of Hebrew and then Greco-Aramaic culture, and that in order to understand what the writers had meant, one had to understand the literary genres (of which historical reporting was only a minor one) in which the Scriptures were written.

My exposure later on to the plurality of religious traditions and to the psychological theories of C. G. Jung refined this lesson. From Jungian thought I learned that religion itself is a literary genre. All mythological language is a literary device intended to elicit experience in the listeners, to alter their states of consciousness so that they see something of what the original seer perceived and so feel their world transformed and layered with mystical significance.

This is, of course, on one level or another, the effort of all literature, and especially poetry. As the poets force us with their images and words to find in ourselves their experiences, so the mystics, prophets, and spokesmen for divine reality urge us with subtle, psychologically active, and powerful symbols to kindle in our hearts what burned in theirs.

Not only are the words of the poets and mystics literary devices, but so also are those of the scientist and historian. Curiously, Father Pieper's rebuke, intended perhaps to admonish me to pursue a greater discipline in my religion, foreshadowed my discovery of the arbitrariness of religious truth, and even of reality itself.

In the summer, after following the admonition of the Advent sermon to leave San Francisco, I stayed for a few months in the Smoky Mountains of North Carolina. I went there to recuperate from the work on the prostitution study, to write, and to help friends construct a meditation hall for Southern Dharma Foundation. We began that job by clearing a site in the midst of the dense woods, which left several enormous piles of brush.

One morning, after meditation in the predawn hours, two of us set out to burn the brush. We were starting early to avoid the day's heat. The fire was blazing, but hardly unmanageable. The smoke that could have been choking shot straight up above the roaring flames into the slowly lightening sky. The warmth felt good in the cool dampness of the mountain morning. The gods were pleased with our sacrifice, I thought whimsically, pleased that soon earnest seekers would come to sit in meditation in these woods, to join the possums and groundhogs in praising life.

As the sun began to peek over the top of the mountain, on whose slope Southern Dharma is built, the fire began to slow its burning and to spread out through the pile of brush. The smoke began to settle around us and sting our eyes. As the sunlight warmed the air above us, I realized, we were losing the draft that had powered our fire and hurled the smoke heavenward. It was a good thing we started early, I thought. I also thought that perhaps the sun god was angry with us, jealous that we'd lit up the sky before he did and so was punishing us by sending the smoke down around us. That was also a way to interpret our experience, as many human beings before had understood just such experiences of their own.

There is more than one reality. We can find realities characterized primarily by causality; we can find those characterized primarily by meaningfulness. The world of the senses shows us only a portion of reality. The world we see does not show us meaning. Meaning is not measured along one of the three spatial dimensions. Meaning exists in the dimension of consciousness. Meaning seems to be projected onto the world from a multidimensional reality beyond.

There is a reality beyond the world we see that offers the meaning that conscious beings want and need. This is the reality described in the myth and metaphor of religion, art, and culture. This reality beyond is not so much an ethereal heaven as it is the matrix for the associations and interconnections that constitute the meaning of experience. The myths and metaphors that describe this transcendent reality are themselves not sacrosanct (though, of course, they are treated as just that). They must be continually adjusted to suit the "real world." In fact, they must be discovered in the experience of the world. The templates and patterns of myth we can learn from the past, but the content must be discovered in our own lives and our own times.

We can choose whether we will see the world as flat and prosaic or as rich and multilayered. We can change how we see our reality. And, in a way we cannot fully understand, because our focus of attention influences the realities we perceive, that changed vision can flow back into the world and reshape it.

Following my own myth led me into a hidden and troubled underside of sexuality in America. It was difficult. It demanded a change in my self-concept. It led me into a world of vice and boredom with which I was unprepared to deal. It caused me anxiety, anguish, foolhardiness, and imprudence. But it forced me to broaden my horizons to seek spiritual insight. And it showed me meaning in the underworld that for so many people seems pruriently alluring but primarily repugnant, and certainly unredeemed.

In the end, part of my discovery was that that world—shot through with sexuality—is so alien and so repugnant because we are generally unable or reluctant to give it meaning. So, weaving together themes from popular culture and from both the esoteric and the mainstream religious traditions and from my own personal experience, I created a tapestry of meaning. I found that the world, held together in its warp and woof, was transformed for me, so that it demonstrated not merely human anguish, but God's love for the world being actively compassionate and harvesting and redeeming human experience.

I made sense of my own experience according to the myth of the hero. In the stories of two great heroes, the world saviors of Mahayana Buddhism and Christianity, I found images of the divine love saving the world, and behind the images clues to a meaning for sexual experience. Perhaps such clues can help us through the present critical moment in consciousness and help us deal responsibly with modern sexuality.

TEN

Virtues for a New Sexuality

All around us sexuality is being openly experienced in non-traditional ways. The appearance of sexually precocious teenagers on urban streets is only one manifestation of the revolution that has occurred in our sexual mores. But the visibility of sex is only a minor aspect of much broader changes in contemporary society. Modern life puts tremendous pressure on what is called the "traditional family"—as though there were anything really traditional about the relatively recently developed nuclear family of husband and wife and two children living hundreds of miles from family roots and support systems.

Ever since the industrial revolution family patterns have been steadily changing. And now the mobility afforded by ease of transportation and demanded by shifts in employment patterns, the influence of scientific rationalism, technology, and mass media, the independence and equality that women have achieved, the cultivation through advertising of new markets, the tremendous rise in the cost of raising a family, the urbanization of American society—all these are changing the way people relate sexually.

These changes in society have had far-reaching effects. Personal space, that is, the areas in life over which one feels control and to which one feels responsibility and commitment, has shrunk from the clan to the nuclear family and now to the individual. This shrinking of the sense of self down to the individual has been termed the modern narcissism. Yet, simultaneously, personal space has expanded to include a vast variety of experiences that were not previously available.

Space and time have changed for us; we travel in a day distances even our recent ancestors would have considered out of the question. We fit more experiences into a year than some of them did into a lifetime. Through the print and electronic media we live vicariously the stories of multitudes of individual lives. We experience our interconnection with the whole world; personal survival is linked to planetary survival. What has changed is the fundamental sense of the person.

What is commonly referred to as a "sexual revolution" may be less a change in behavior—there have always been fornicators and adulterers—than an increase in the willingness of people to be open, honest, and guiltless about their enjoyment of sex. Many sexually active individuals, far from considering themselves fornicators or adulterers, see themselves as pioneers of a new and humanistic morality.

To some, conventional beliefs about sex and natural law seem outdated, but this does not mean there can be no moral guidelines for modern-day sex. Old ideas about virtuous sexuality, especially that sex was primarily for procreation within a monogamous marriage, are no longer relevant to many people, but this does not mean the new sexuality must be devoid of virtue. Indeed, perhaps the greatest challenge for ethical thinkers is to develop an ethics for contemporary sexual behavior.

Today's psychologically sophisticated society is founded on faith in the "perfectibility of man." Those whom Toby Marotta called liberationists found that their self-actualizing "live and let live," "go with the flow" values effectively reconciled liberty and freedom of self-expression for individuals with harmony and cooperation among people, and, in fact, seemed to result in successful and psychologically healthy lives for themselves and for others.

Despite the arguments of contemporary preachers of the Religious Right, such humanism is neither un-American nor, for that matter, un-Christian. Jefferson, Franklin, and the men who framed the Declaration of Independence and the Constitution were anticlerical Deists who believed that humankind's duty to God was to develop human values. They believed in pluralism and individual freedom. They created America as an experiment in democracy, freedom, and humanism. Such humanism is remarkably close to the teachings of Jesus himself, who, also anticlerical, called for human beings to work out problems not by creating ecclesiastical law or by expecting divine interventions, but by developing fundamentally human qualities of interpersonal love and respect.

One reason so many moderns are skeptical of institutionalized Christianity is that it opposes the notion of the perfectibility of humankind (and, consequently, democratic process). Such opposition seems to be the real basis for the objection to biological evolution. To the popular mind, evolution suggests that humankind is gradually improving. Fundamentalist Christianity resists that faith in human nature, focusing instead on the evil and unruliness of the human heart and subsequent need for a redeemer. What is considered important to Christian Creationists is less the historicity of the creation account in Genesis than the story of the fall. Curiously, however, such concern with the fall and with the darkness of the heart seems to contradict the Christian "good news" of Redemption. Jesus Christ, the gospel proclaimed, has taken away the sin of the world.

The notion that the world is inherently evil is clearly counterproductive. As religion scholar Huston Smith comments in *Beyond the Post-Modern Mind,* ". . . the hypothesis that this is a good world and fuller understanding will carry us beyond appearances to the contrary is the most fruitful working hypothesis there is, comparable in metaphysics to science's working premise that cancer has a cause even if it is not yet known. . . ."

An ethics for the modern sexual life must support the individual's freedom to choose his or her own modes of personal fulfillment, while offering guidelines for responsible behavior that improve relationships and help overcome the boredom and anomie that dehumanizes so much of life. Then, instead of confirming the evil of the world, it assists us in creating a good world in which to live.

The sexual revolution grew up with the counterculture of the late 1960s and '70s. In many ways the counterculture was an ethical and social reform movement. It sought to vindicate pleasure and to place the experience of pleasure in a loving, interpersonal context. What was important about countercultural ethics was less its blasé attitude toward sex and drugs than its demand for personal freedom and truth-telling. Be true to yourself, the hippies said, fulfill your own destiny; don't just do what convention tells you. Truth-telling demanded that sex be acknowledged explicitly and not camouflaged with latinate euphemisms and that pleasure be recognized as the obvious good everyone experiences it to be but has been taught to deny neurotically.

This countercultural sensibility championed self-actualization and respect for diversity. Its new morality rejects traditional notions of sinfulness and rules that are obeyed mainly because they are attached to threats of eternal damnation. Today, self-actualization and interpersonal fulfillment are the only valid reasons for obeying codes of conduct not directly enforced by the police. Self-actualization means behaving out of a sense of responsibility to oneself, to one's fellow humans, and to one's sense of God, not out of fear that that God will hurl one into an imaginary fire pit.

Countercultural thought championed the democratization of values. Realizing that rules governing the pursuit of pleasure are far more human-made than God-given, counterculturalists insisted that good should be determined according to what people really do, not what a few preachers and moral guardians proclaim is good for others. They recognized that aristocrats and rich, well-educated, and successful individuals have always been sexually and socially free and that traditional taboos and social conventions frequently worked simply to prevent the less privileged and fortunate from enjoying similar freedoms. Finding that progress had created a large affluent and educated class, they proclaimed that it was time the privilege of the few be extended to the many.

Now, in the '80s, we can see that the changes in attitudes and in human consciousness that sparked the rise of the counterculture have affected sexual behavior of all kinds. It is not that contemporary society has discovered new forms of sex, but that its emphasis on openness, explicitness, and freedom has made available to the masses options they would rarely have considered previously, or enjoyed only covertly, guiltily, and with greater likelihood of harm, irresponsibility, and distortion.

With this democratization of new freedoms, new problems have arisen. Sexual exploitation of children, to the extent it really exists, is but one sign of our difficulties in adjusting to new freedoms and new values. Yet that this subject can now be recognized, investigated, and dealt with openly is one of the benefits of the changes in attitudes about sex.

What is perhaps at the root of all these changes in sexual attitudes is the notion that sex need not be exclusively for reproduction. In the Christian past, sex had no other function than procreation; sexual pleasure was considered vulgar. Even the desire for "carnal relations" was sinful. One was not supposed to think about sex. One was certainly not supposed to fantasize sexual experiences or to stimulate oneself sexually with those fantasies. Today, sex is beginning to be recognized—especially by psychologists—as, in itself, a good for individuals, not simply a function for social survival.

The development of effective contraceptives has forced all of us to recognize that, for most people, sex *is* good in and of itself. Indeed, were it not for religious indoctrination, most people probably wouldn't understand what the moralistic objections are all about. When we decline to restrict sex to reproduction, then masturbation, extramarital sex, non-vaginal intercourse, and even homosexuality cease to be real issues. People may still have biases against unconventional sex, but the rationale for them is gone.

Paradoxically, engaging in sex outside the reproductive context has often been called indulging our animal nature. It is precisely the opposite. Animal nature is to copulate instinctively only to produce progeny. As Jacob Bronowski observed, what is natural for human beings is certainly not behavior that is found also in animals, but what is different and unique to humans. Human beings, of course, feel the instinct to produce progeny, but that is only a part of our sexual experience. (Our over-populated world proves we needn't fear that condoning non-procreative sex will threaten racial survival.) Precisely the way we differ from animals that have rigid sexual cycles and less involving and less orgasmic intercourse is that human sexual contact involves consciousness and volition.

We have been taught to accept as normal, even virtuous, behavior toward a sexual partner we'd never tolerate toward anyone else. Today old norms for relationship appear, too often, to have become justifications for neurotic traits. Monogamy may be nothing more than institutionalized jealousy and possessiveness; indissolubility of marriage only institutionalized fear of change. Instead of supporting love and relationship, the old norms seem simply to create additional pressures. One of the reasons old norms seem outdated is that they have lost their context.

The concern for self-actualization and social harmony places sexual ethics in the context of interpersonal relationships, not natural law or traditional social custom. In such a context it is clear, for instance, that unconventional sex engaged in by an unmarried couple who respect and care for one another is not necessarily sinful and that missionary position vaginal intercourse imposed on an unwilling, unsatisfied woman by a bored, but horny husband is not necessarily virtuous. John Paul II seems to have been trying to make a similar point when he declared early in his papacy that a husband can lust sinfully in his heart even after his own wife. Unfortunately John Paul's effort to focus on the quality of relationship got tripped up by the Roman tradition's impossible position of considering sinful not only acts but thoughts about the acts. Thus rather than to praise love and respect in relationship, his comments were taken to demean sex further.

The religions have, of course, traditionally demeaned sex. But perhaps the real message in this is that sex and love are indeed separable. The love that we are urged to feel for other beings by the spiritual teachers is not simply the neurotic attachment we call "falling in love," with all the emotions of jealousy, insecurity, and obsession that involves. The compulsions of such adolescent sexual attraction must not be mistaken for virtue. Falling in love is a delightful and educational experience we should not refuse ourselves, but it must not be taken for all there is to love or sex.

The spiritual traditions have warned that sexual urges can mire individuals and societies in egoistic concerns. That warning wasn't against sex but against ego. Suppressing sex doesn't necessarily free either individuals or societies from ego. In fact, according to Freudian theory, it simply shifts energy to other egoistic concerns, some of them much more antisocial—competitiveness, acquisitiveness, and belligerence. What has to change in each of us isn't our interest in sex, but our fearful, irresponsible, dishonest, and self-obsessed approaches to sexual behavior. What we must overcome is not our bodies' need for pleasure, affection, and touch, but our egos' tendency to be neurotic, compulsive, insecure, and self-centered.

Perhaps the religious condemnations of sex are really warnings about the pitfalls of sex-linked neuroses. Perhaps people have been urged to be non-sexual, or at least restricted in their sexuality, because erotic desire can spark the neuroses of jealousy, possessiveness, manipulativeness, and covertness. We are told *agape* should supplant *eros. Agape* does not necessarily restrict behavior. It should open us up so that we can love more. It should transform our experience of life and of *eros.*

The sexual revolution, in part, arose from a moral sensibility that championed *agape,* that rejected old rules that seemed more concerned with maintaining power for the Churches than with teaching individuals to be free and responsible. After all, sexual behavior should manifest attractive, self-actualizing traits. Primary human virtues, like love, kindness, generosity, respect, selflessness, patience, and not notions of ownership or of politeness, legality, decorum, or social convenience should characterize sexual behavior.

From my earliest experience of the counterculture while I was still in religious life, I understood that this modern sensibility inspired "operative virtues"—that is, behavior characteristics that manifested its assumptions and values. I called these operative virtues wonder, innocence, transparency, gentleness, adventure, and pluralism. Wonder is at the base of all of them. For the counterculture believed that life was wonderful and supremely sacred; that was why nobody should hurt anyone else or restrict anyone's experience of life.

The new sexuality, because it also champions freedom and self-actualization, actually implies similar virtues. In fact, the virtues suggested by both the counterculture and the new sexuality seem to parallel traditional virtues of the spiritual life.

Poverty of things and possessions, poverty of spirit, disinterest, non-attachment, surrender—all have been proclaimed as essential to the growth of the spirit. Despite the fact that ownership is a foundation of our culture, concern with ownership is not an attractive trait. It's ugly in a toddler screaming, "mine, mine," and it's uglier in an adult shouting rudely at someone who's picked up a pen to write with or leaned against a car while waiting for the bus: "Hey, don't touch that—it's mine!"

The spiritual recommendation of poverty has come out of the

tradition of repudiation of the world and abnegation of the ego. It also comes out of the life-affirming insight expressed in the jingle by San Francisco bohemian holy man Joe Miller:

Everything is floating and everyone is free;
There's nothing I can call mine, 'cause everything is me.

This is perhaps what Jesus meant in saying: "Blessed are the poor in spirit; they shall possess the earth."

We can't own the things that matter to us. And trying to make the things we can own matter smothers the soul. We can't own truth. In the charming image of the medieval German mystic Meister Eckhart, we can't throw a tablecloth over God and haul him home to keep under the kitchen table for our exclusive use. And, in the same way, we can't own other people. We can't hold on to them; we can't make them agree with us or do what we say. The old laws that considered females property don't make sense today. The idea of ownership and possession has no proper application in interpersonal relationships.

The Buddhists use the word "non-clinging" for this attitude of poverty and respect for others. Non-clinging calls for abjuration of self-righteousness, dogmatism, conviction, bigotry, certitude, egotism, and self-aggrandizement. It amounts to openness to experience and willingness to change. Non-clinging is the basis for making sexual relationships uncommitted and open. As Joe Miller's jingle continues:

So don't you try to hold on to anyone you know,
Just feel the life within you and let the changes flow.

Vulnerability—the willingness, in Jesus' words, to take up one's cross, to say "not my will, but thine," to accept life as it comes—is essentially openness to change, to adventure, and to involvement. Being vulnerable means dropping masks and barriers. It can mean letting ourselves "fall in love" when we find beauty and excitement and responsiveness in another person. When we are vulnerable our sexuality can draw us into relationship.

Vulnerability is also the basis for creating lasting relationships that are maintained less because of legal and social commitments than because of interpersonal involvement and concern. Vulnerability may imply practical monogamy. At least, it implies a care to protect our intimate relationships, to nurture them as we would a newborn life. It is to make ourselves as vulnerable as such a newborn. That means being innocent, risking a loss of control over our lives and feelings, allowing others to enter in and gain power and influence. It may mean trusting—even with the possibility of getting hurt.

The virtue of vulnerability requires that we reach out to others, allow ourselves to be hurt, protect our relationships, and allow our Beloveds to maintain a deep and special place in our hearts. Vulnerability means gracing all our relationships with a care that they never be lost, that time may change but will not destroy them. The pilgrimage of life may lead us away from a Beloved, but the ties can remain.

Our languages are full of words and stock phrases that we all use freely, but which often mean different things to different people. A necessary virtue, called for by psychological sophistication, is understanding. We must listen to and understand those whose lives intersect ours. We must recognize that their universe is different from ours and, though we may not always like what we hear from them, we must affirm their point of view and struggle to understand what they are saying from their perspective. And we must remember that our sexual urges, because they arise from the unconscious, can cloud our understanding, and so we must be especially generous and gentle with those for whom we have sexual feelings.

* * *

Proponents of the new sexuality pride themselves on being realistic. Modern life puts enormous pressures on sex, love, and relationship. The old supports are gone. We have to create new models of relationship for ourselves.

Sexual meeting has become casual. For singles, initial sexual interest may be the start of important, but often subsequently nonsexual, relationships. What was once condemned as promiscuity is now becoming the norm of social recreation for many. And the openness to sexual encounter no longer seems describable as promiscuity, with its connotations of furtiveness, sinfulness, and compulsiveness.

The norm of monogamy was the single, indissoluble, heterosexual relationship. Designed in great part to assure stability for child-rearing, it gloried in the intensity that love can develop in a life committed to only one other person. The new promiscuity, which is hardly new, having been a feature of urban life probably since the rise of cities in ancient times, glories in wide-ranging experience, skill in interpersonal relating, and individual autonomy. Its goal is self-actualization.

It would be naive to claim that all sexually active moderns are fulfilled persons skilled at relating (as it would be that all married couples are happy and loving). But for many, and even among those who choose to marry, raise a family, and maybe move to the suburbs or the country, actualization of personal potentials, including sexual and intimate emotional potentials, is a more salient goal than conventional conjugal bliss. Few members of the modern American couple refer to their spouses or partners as "my other half."

In the world in which relationship is not guaranteed by constraints of monogamy and permanence, we may have to deal with our Beloveds' sexual interest in another person or their desire simply to enjoy the freedom available to them because of contemporary sexual mores, or their loss of interest in us and desire to move on to another relationship. And we have to be realistic. For we all can be, and have been, both Lover and Beloved. We've wronged and been wronged. We've fallen out of love first or never fallen in love at all; we've been rejected or had our love go unrequited. We've felt the allure of sexual freedom and spontaneity. And so we understand (comprehend) that we can do nothing else but understand (accept and agree to).

It is difficult to accept that the Beloved no longer desires us (that has in at least one instance been an ongoing source of pain in my own life) or desires another. But failing to understand accomplishes nothing, whereas understanding, being willing to listen and care unselfishly, to wish the Beloved new love and more joy, makes us more lovable, may renew our Beloved's perceptions of the goodness that once inspired the Beloved's love, and makes us bigger and happier even in the face of our loss.

When we understand, we may not be able to change anything in the Beloved's decision, but we may find we can keep the love and affection. We can maintain a relationship of mutual trust and support for the day when the demands of erotic excitement have cooled and the comfort of shared experience and accumulation of years have come to seem more important. Then, as we move in and out of relationships, we need not be leaving behind a wake of hate and spoiled lives, but instead be making investments in trust and understanding for our collective futures.

The anxiety that a loved one feels about a Beloved's encounter, even a single one, with a competitor is based on the fallacy—a holdover from the old monogamy—of "compulsive coupling." We have been taught to worry that our Beloved will totally forget who we are, what goodness we have shown, and what joy we have shared. But that is simply not the case. Human beings— especially males—have an urge for novelty and adventure, but they don't have the need to flit from relationship to relationship. Almost all of us have seen that few of those we become infatuated with, and even fewer of those we lust after, would we want to keep as lovers.

The reason a person might fall into the pattern of compulsive coupling, leaving one relationship for another simply because of a sexual experience outside the relationship, is that the relationship was too stifling in the first place. Confronted, as we are, with the dazzle of sexual freedom, one of the most realistic functions of a primary relationship is to provide mutual support in exploring the variety that is available. Perhaps the greatest accomplishment of the new sexual ethics is that it frees us, at least in theory, from having to choose between the excluding options of absolute monogamy and compulsive, dissolute, and furtive promiscuity.

Every relationship creates agreements (and these may seem very traditional) that are morally binding—not so much because of sexual morality as because of the sacredness of agreements. The virtues of non-clinging and understanding are not justifications for infidelity to agreements, but they are realistic solutions to what are common difficulties in human relationships, regardless of the agreements made. Such solutions, based on positive virtuous attitudes instead of restrictive rules, may serve to save relationships in the long run and to transform neurotic obsessions that rot the soul into opportunities for spiritual and psychological growth.

Understanding one another, understanding human nature, feeling compassion for ourselves and others, we can invest with virtue all the styles of sexuality and in doing so we can transform our own vision and we can transform the world. The new sexuality is simply a new arena in which to work out our salvation with diligence. If, after all, the work of the spiritual life is to feel compassion for others and to overcome selfishness and ego, then the practice of non-clinging and understanding can provide all the self-abnegation and compassion we could possibly want.

More important than maintaining the conventions of the last century is developing responsible patterns of sexual behavior adaptive to modern life. For the necessary correlate of our modern freedom is responsibility. Without responsibility freedom soon evaporates. Such responsibility is very practical. It demands that we pay attention to the consequences of our behavior.

One practical responsibility of those who relate sexually to a variety of partners, even if only very occasionally, is to observe good health practices. A major problem of sexual freedom is the spread of sexually transmitted diseases. With the sexual revolution the incidence of such diseases seems to have increased, though it is not clear whether what has increased is the incidence of the diseases or the honest reporting and attention paid to them. Diseases have appeared that have heretofore been rare. Awareness of them should stimulate people to evaluate just what is responsible sexual behavior. (Particularly among gay men, in part because their subculture is now self-aware and organized, the spread of Acquired Immune Deficiency Syndrome (AIDS) has caused many to reconsider the styles of liberated sex and to work together to help end this threat to national health.)

A second practical responsibility for both men and women is to prevent unwanted pregnancies and to accept the life commitment that pregnancy implies. There is no unqualified right to reproduce. Some people simply do not have the ability to provide a life of quality for offspring.

If there are villains of the sexual underworld that is full of runaway children who've been sexually and physically abused, forced to run to the streets, and there bought and sold for sex, it is the parents who brought these kids into the world without the intention and commitment to care for them. If a change in society is needed, it is to free people from the notion that they must have children to be worthwhile. If laws are needed, they should be against incest and child abuse, not against family planning and abortion. These are, after all, ways of exercising reproductive responsibility. And the exercise of such responsibility is ultimately virtuous and life-affirming.

What epitomizes the failure of society, under the influence of religion, to champion reproductive responsibility is the Roman

Church's condemnation of contraception. But, ironically, what has become a purely juridical commandment, and the source of much contention, was originally intended to be a spiritual affirmation of life and of embodiment. As historical theologian John Noonan shows in his book *Contraception,* while the Christian position has been complex, the Roman condemnation primarily derived from objections by the Fathers of the Church to dualistic life-denying Gnostic doctrines of sexuality and, most importantly, from the recriminations against Manichaeism by Augustine of Hippo.

Manichaeism was an intensely dualistic religion born of Zoroastrianism, Gnosticism, Christianity, and perhaps even Buddhism. It taught that, because conception imprisons spirit in matter, procreation is evil. Consistant with that, Manichaeism was antisexual, but its objection was mainly to reproduction. Indeed, some Manichaeans believed that sexual ecstasy (and the ritual eating of semen) could release spirit from its prison. And not all Manichaeans were prepared to renounce sex altogether. Thus they recommended contraceptive practice. (Ironically, Noonan observes, that practice was the one birth control method that centuries later the Roman Church would consider acceptable: rhythm.)

Saint Augustine, and after him the Church, objected to the Manichaean doctrine that the flesh was inherently evil. After all, the material world had been redeemed by Christ's Incarnation and Self-sacrifice. What was at stake in the controversy was the efficacy of the Redemption. Augustine proposed that procreation of new life in the flesh was good. But Augustine was a convert from Manichaeism and he demonstrated the convert's zeal to renounce the past while at the same time continuing to manifest it. Thus, still a dualist at heart, he did not recognize sexual pleasure, however integral to the whole experience, as equally good. He maintained that procreation was the only valid purpose for sex, and that sexual pleasure should be minimized.

From the condemnation of the Manichaeans through that of the medieval Cathars (who, in the courtly love tradition, resurrected Manichaean ideas) down to the present day, the Roman Church's prohibition of contraception has seemed almost anything but life- and sex-positive. Yet what has always marked the Church's stance has been an intent to affirm the goodness and beauty of human life and the sanctity of the flesh. In fact, recently the Church's objection has not been to sex as much as to artificial interference in natural life processes. But because it exercises responsibility contraceptive practice can be positively life-affirming.

The simplest and least artificial form of contraception is avoidance of intravaginal ejaculation. One way to accomplish this that requires virtually no preparation is the practice of *coitus obstructus,* or *karezza,* as it was called by John Humphrey Noyes of the Oneida Community, which practiced it routinely.* There are many sexual styles that will not result in conception, including, of course, homosexuality which Carl Jung, among many others, thought was a natural population control. Recent surveys, like that of Shere Hite, have suggested that, while coitus may be included in sex play, many heterosexual couples find that alternative means of stimulation, particularly mutual masturbation, not only avoid conception, but can be more orgasmically satisfying for the female and less psychologically pressuring for the male.

If sex is only sometimes intended for reproduction, then accidents that result in conception ought to be correctable. Thus abortion can be another means of exercising reproductive responsibility. But abortion raises many issues. Most of the arguments both for and against abortion are simply red herrings.

---

*Pressure exerted at the base of the scrotum will divert a male's semen into the bladder. Even though this practice is clumsy and not foolproof, it is curious that almost no one I've asked has ever even heard of *coitus obstructus!*

Neither "a woman's right to control her own body" nor "the moment life begins" really mean anything in the concrete. None of us really control our own bodies; and life is hardly so quantifiable that we can say it has a specific beginning. Both the control over one's own body and the beginning of life are spread along continuums, and the morality of abortion must be dealt with on a case-by-case basis.

The problem with abortion lies not in the morality of individual acts, but in the general effect on a society of casually destroying new life. For, after all, whether fetuses are "alive" or not, pregnancy itself is a powerful symbol in consciousness of the conquest of life over death, of the continuation of the transpersonal Self despite the demise of individuals. Irresponsible abortion is socially demoralizing, not life-affirming. It does not demonstrate the freedom that the sexual revolution has championed, but the failure to accept that freedom. What we must create, however, are not new laws or moral principles to prevent abortion, but virtue and vision to see beyond the individual ego to the collective. What is really at issue in the question of abortion, and in the question of sexual freedom in general, is the responsibility of the living to create a world of quality for the not-yet-living.

Even those who are happily settled in relationships or for whom the new sexual freedom means very little share the responsibilities. Responsibility begins in the home. Parents have an obligation to teach their children about sexually transmitted diseases and the hygiene to reduce risk of exposure the same way they teach them about measles, chicken pox, and colds. They have an obligation to explain sex and contraception the same way they teach religion and morality.

The institutions of society have an obligation to make certain that children are given sound and intelligent information about sex, even when parents are remiss. The children belong to all of us. They are our future, whether we sire and birth them ourselves or only pay the taxes to provide them schools and—if none of us begins to act responsibly—to pay for their abortions or to support their accidental families.

As a society, we have a responsibility to solve the problems of unwanted pregnancies and sexually transmitted diseases through social planning and medical research. Politicians and civic leaders are sometimes reluctant to support such causes, fearing that it will be taken as approval of unconventional sex. Religious leaders oppose solutions to the problems, suggesting that misfortune and disease are punishments from God. But unconventional sex is real and won't go away, and the punishment seems to fall on the good and the evil alike. We all suffer because of unwanted pregnancies and irresponsible abortions. Venereal diseases affect us all whether or not we're exposed to the contagion directly. Because the antibiotics with which most of them are treated enter the life cycle of the whole planet, their widespread use speeds up the development of resistant strains—not only of sexually transmitted diseases—but of all virulent bacteria.

More than anything else, individually and collectively we have a responsibility to pay attention to how our attitudes about sex affect our world. As we've seen, problems such as that of juvenile prostitution are only exacerbated by sex-negative attitudes and misinformed interventions.

In the end what most graces all sexual experience and relationship is an attitude that makes no behavioral demands, but may, in fact, result in all the virtues. This is the virtue of gladness.

Sex may not always be entered into happily. Sometimes it seems a desperate grappling to escape loneliness. Sometimes it seems a duty that must be fulfilled in order to assure other benefits. Sometimes there is an undercurrent of anger and resentment (that for some may even seem to increase the pleasure of the physical release). And sometimes there is a great sadness and poignancy that surrounds lovemaking.

Sex is the source and focus of much of the pain in our lives. Our love of those to whom we feel attracted raises us up, but also casts us down. Our sexuality mars our motivation and causes us endless distress. Our concern for how others judge us traps us in ego.

Even so, if our sexual activity is going to lead us beyond ego into participation with the divine creative activity, if it is going to enhance our lives and keep us young and vital as we grow mature and wise, we must feel glad that it remains ever present in our consciousness. We must acknowledge it and not pretend that it isn't really there; we must affirm it, recognizing how it grants us roots into transpersonal dimensions of reality.

And we must feel glad for others that they too can experience the joy and delight. What will transform our vision is our gladness for others' sexuality. All too often religion has made people feel guilty, resentful, and disapproving. In the name of religion other people are condemned, their sex is made vulgar, their joy denied. That attitude has not created the Kingdom of Heaven on earth, but a hell, ruled over by self-righteous bigots. The problems of the sexual underworld are but one manifestation of this hell.

It is not easy and demands deliberate struggle, but we must change that. If we want to save the world we must remind ourselves frequently to feel glad. We can feel glad that there are beautiful men and women in our world. We can feel glad for them when we see other people caught up in one another's sexual spell. We can support one another's loving relationships. We can feel glad and not resentful or disapproving when we learn of others' sexual experience. We can stop snickering embarrassedly about sex and begin proclaiming its goodness. We can affirm the goodness of embodied life.

We must be glad, detached from the superficial forms and

appearances, that we are alive and that our life generates more life, both in the wombs of the mothers of our children and in the experiential universe created by the interaction of the multitude of conscious beings. So that, recalling our divine origins, we may look on all that we have made and see that it is very good.

ELEVEN

The Resurrection
of the Body

All of us know that what is real is what is physical. Unless we can get a physical sense of something, it just isn't real. We don't believe in it if it can't be manifested either in some thing or in the behavior of some thing or some person. Thus the religious and mythological traditions have always used physical manifestations—sacrament, ritual, and meditative visualization—to convey the spirit.

The myths reveal that the multiple layers of reality are all continuous with and contained within our own bodies. That too is behind the Christian myth of the resurrection of the body: we take our bodies with us into the Kingdom, for the Kingdom is in the body. It is not somewhere or sometime else. It is how we see the world we live in, how we transform our senses.

His body was "his mind's present image of itself," wrote Arthur C. Clarke of the newly gestated Star-Child in his *2001: A Space Odyssey.* Isn't that true of all of us all the time? Our bodies are our minds' images of ourselves. Our bodies are how we experience ourselves. Our bodies are our way of locating the various functions of consciousness and of extending experience into three-dimensional space.

Meditative systems frequently superimpose the macrocosm of the many-layered universe onto the microcosm of the individual body. Primitive shamanistic meditation leads the initiate in trance to experience dismemberment, evisceration, and reconstruction of the body with objects, like quartz crystal, that are believed to possess spirit power. The Kabbala presents the Sephiroth, the levels of manifesting being, as "organs" of the body of the perfected, transpersonal being, Adam Kadmon, so that meditators can locate these mystical organs in their own bodies. Astrological imagery correlates areas of the anatomy with the zodiacal influences so that adherents can find their physiques visited, and perhaps renewed, organ by organ, as the sun passes through the year, constellation by constellation.

Indian and Tibetan mythology teaches that our physical bodies *(anna-maya-kosa)* are but the densest of five sheaths which crystallize from and around our consciousness. Interpenetrating them and becoming finer and more subtle are the sheaths of our vital or breath bodies *(prana-maya-kosa),* personality or thought bodies *(mano-maya-kosa),* consciousness or spiritual bodies *(vi jñana-maya-kosa),* and universal consciousness or bliss bodies *(ananda-maya-kosa).* The physical body, nourished by food and enlivened by breath, though the most limited and spatially and temporally bound, is penetrated by all the other bodies. It is the link between heaven and earth, the "sacrament" by which personality, depth consciousness, and enlightened bliss are manifested in the world of experience.

A variation on that mythology in *kundalini* and *tantra* yoga describes power centers in the body, called *chakras,* that correlate both with physiological nerve plexuses and with psychological states of consciousness. Chakra meditation focuses on these energy centers in order to open the energy flow throughout the whole mind-body system. Such meditation is believed to improve the working of the body as well as to enlighten the mind. By locating the functions of consciousness within the body, the system of chakras reveals the body as a surface in three dimensions of a being far more complex and dimensionally extended.

The system of chakras appears in various myth systems all around the world. (It is what is represented, for instance, by the familiar medical symbol of the caduceus.) In recent years it has received attention in the West. Especially because it places the sexual functions on a continuum with the psychological and the spiritual, it forms the basis of many current discussions of sex and spirituality.

I first learned of the chakras from Dr. Kim McKell, a Jungian psychologist. Later I learned a technique for focusing on them from Adolphine Carol, a meditation teacher in San Francisco. Adolphine, slightly older than me, has a boyish look and charm that make her curiously ageless. She's been an actress and a producer of TV shows and commercials. She's always been a little psychic. Some years ago, bored with TV production, she took a course at the Berkeley Psychic Institute. She discovered her intuition was often uncannily accurate and her practice of psychic meditation healing and transforming. After completing the full course of studies at B.P.I. she began teaching on her own.

The Institute does not seem to produce the crackpots its name might suggest. Adolphine seemed to have an open-minded and intelligent approach to the psychic world. I was always surprised and pleased to find how sanely she spoke of such odd-ball topics as pyramidology, aura reading, spirit guides, UFO's, and the like —topics I'd heard too often as signs of incipient psychoses. I had come to understand these psychic and pseudo-scientific phenomena as metaphors for experiences of alternate realities. But I'd seen that, like the metaphors of myth and religion, some people took these metaphors literally. Adolphine appeared to have found in herself and her own spiritual process a way of passing right over the bizarre exterior to the symbolic truth beyond.

In teaching the chakra meditation Adolphine ignored the complex Vedic and Hindu mythologies and esoteric symbols. *Kundalini* and *tantric* practices, I had heard, could be powerful and even dangerous. The Indian holy man and British civil servant Gopi Krishna reported that his unprepared practice of the meditations left him anoretic and virtually schizophrenic for years. Adolphine's method seemed simpler and safer precisely because it avoided the techniques and breath practices that could unleash the torrent of neurological activity called the *kundalini.*

Her method worked simply to normalize energy flow, activating the potential levels of awareness in a smooth rhythm.

Adolphine led her students, usually eight to ten at a time, in guided meditations on energy flow. She suggested visualizing the energy as movement of color through channels in the body, and, holding up a telescoping vegetable steamer from her kitchen to illustrate, she suggested visualizing the chakras as valves that open and close to control the flow through these channels. The aim is to be able to open and close them appropriately, even intentionally.

Encrustations develop on the chakras that block control and result in neurotic traits (fears, obsessions, rages, denial, and the like) that prevent people from fully experiencing life. As we visualized each chakra and the emotional/intellectual state associated with it, Adolphine explained, the blocks would surface as memories, distractions, or fantasies. The blocks could be opened by observing them and running energy through them, thus "discharging" and "grounding" them.

Over a period of weeks, Adolphine taught us how to localize consciousness in the center of the head and ground ourselves so that our thoughts were not being constantly tugged at by outside concerns, then to attend to energy moving through us, and to visualize the seven major chakras along the spine and the minor chakras in the hands and feet (which are the basis of palmistry and foot reflexology). She taught us to be aware of ourselves not merely as bodies stuck in space and time but as energy beings, in fact, able to move in time by means of memory and anticipation; in space by way of imagination; and in consciousness by visualization and intentionality.

"At the base of the spine," she explained, "is the first chakra. This chakra controls the simplest, most primitive, and often autonomic aspect of the person. Here are the survival mechanisms of the body: metabolism, immunity, and the will to live. When energy is blocked here you feel insecure, threatened, diseased, desperately grasping for food, for goods, for attention, and sure that there must be a scarcity of such things. When the chakra is closed down, you feel uptight and compulsive; when it is open all the way, scattered and out of control.

"The second chakra is at the level of the genitals. Here are your primary pleasure centers. Here the body joins with other bodies in direct chakra-to-chakra contact. Here infatuation and erotic relationship, as well as procreation of new life are controlled. From the second chakra are also regulated endocrine functions: the juices that keep you young-looking, attractive, vital, and appealing to others. When the chakra is closed down you look and feel unattractive, the body ages and affections wither, the thought of other people making love seems repulsive. When it is open all the way, you are buffeted about by sexual urges and compulsions, your emotions seem out of control and your behavior unpleasantly outrageous. When the chakra is operating smoothly you feel sensuously alive, attracted and attractive, responsive to other people's affections. Encrustations on the chakra may be experienced as guilt or as memories of parents or authorities telling you to behave yourself or as obsessions with sexual images or compulsions toward fetishes.

"The third chakra is located in the solar plexus. Here are your emotional and motivational centers. Here you experience rage and ambition, as well as fright and 'butterflies in the stomach.' When the chakra is closed down you feel timid and weak, impotent and feckless. When it is open all the way, you feel irrationally confident or strong, driven by anger or competition. When the chakra is functioning smoothly you have all the get up and go you need as well as the control over your emotions.

"The fourth chakra is located in the heart. Here the energies of the lower chakras are transformed by love and compassion and carried up into the spiritual and intellectual realms. When the heart is closed, the lower passions drive you. Concerns of security, pleasure, and power dominate consciousness. When the heart is totally open you lose your identity in the oneness with humankind, and you may become nonfunctional. When the chakra is functioning smoothly you remain aware of yourself and your feelings, but you also feel involved with other people. You can love and be loved.

"The fifth chakra is in the throat. Here are located in the thyroid the function of controlling metabolism and in the larynx of speaking to other people. The chakra is associated with discipline, especially religious discipline and ritual, and with teaching and communication. Communication is the major way of shaping your environment and discipline is your way of shaping yourself to fit your environment. When the fifth chakra is closed down, you may feel inarticulate and tongue-tied; you may seem obsessed with rituals—from Church services to neurotic compulsions—but unable to understand what the rituals are for. When the chakra is opened totally, you may find yourself talking uncontrollaby, rambling tactlessly, unable to discipline yourself and resenting others' discipline; the fact that people enjoy going to church, for example, might seem galling. When the chakra is functioning properly you are able to communicate openly and tell the truth; you are secure in your ability to perform your duties and you can profit from social rituals and religious practices.

"The sixth chakra is located in the center of your head. Here your experiential world is created. Through the eyes and ears, primarily, enters the information on which you base experience; in the way you sort that information your universe is created. Here also, through your 'third eye,' spiritual sight is experienced. When the chakra is closed down you feel a victim of the world you see, unable to take any responsibility for what happens; the world seems desolate and two-dimensional; time seems to drag on; nothing is pleasurable. When the chakra is open all the way you feel ecstatic, but spaced-out, deluded into thinking you can control the universe for your whims; you may feel prideful and self-righteous. When the chakra is functioning properly you see the beauty of the world and you perceive it as the figure against the ground of divine being; you can realize the attractiveness and splendor of the physical world and the multiplicity of worlds that coexist with it.

"The seventh chakra, called the 'thousand-petalled lotus,' is located a few inches above the top of your head. Here God sits as in ancient Hebrew tradition YHWH sat on the extended wings of cherubim atop the Ark of the Convenant. Here is your connection with the One Being who lives the life in all and who sees through your perspective. When the chakra is closed down there is no energy entering your body from above. You are alive but life seems a burden. There is nothing to do but eat, excrete, and reproduce; and the work you have to do to accomplish these makes it all seem worthless. When the chakra is open totally you, as a separate entity, are gone; your perspective disappears and you may simply discorporate and turn into light. Then you end the game and your universe dissipates; your perspective is lost to God. In moments of mystical rapture you may feel blessed that the chakra has opened, but you should remember in those times to stay grounded so that you don't discorporate. When the chakra is functioning properly you feel light and easy in life, detached from taking worries too seriously, but prudent in your affairs, realizing how precious life is and what a treasure you possess and cherish. Only perhaps at the moment of death, when all the chakras are tired and you have exhausted this perspective, will you want to open the seventh chakra fully and gratefully return the life you were given. You should remember this experience, associating it with thoughts of a good death, so that when the time comes you can do it for real."

Traditionally, Western religious life has been based on vows of poverty, chastity, and obedience—that is, surrender of material security, sexual pleasure, and personal will. These are the issues of the first three chakras. The vows were intended to divinize these issues. And the way to do that is to see them through the love and compassion of the heart. The first three chakras are mirrored in the heart as the upper three chakras, as discipline, creative vision, and spiritual security.

The heart is the pivot. It controls how we value the world around us, whether we love it or resent it. It controls how we value the experience of life and of our plurality of selves, whether we deny the range of the chakras, focusing (for the venal and profligate) only on the lower three, or (for the abstracted, spaced-out, or moralistic) only on the higher. It is from the heart that God utters the divine assessment: it is good.

Adolphine's meditation reminds us that life is multi-faceted and that it takes all the chakras smoothly opening and closing with the flow of energy to make our lives. The goal of meditating on this fundamentally sexual energy, called *kundalini,* is to sacramentalize the experience of being embodied so that the physical manifests the spiritual and the spiritual perceives itself and acts in the physical.

Finding spiritual vision in the sexual underworld, for me, meant discovering how to place all my experience along that channel of energy that is my life, learning how to discharge the pain and the problems and to feel intelligent and informed compassion for those who live in that world. It meant balancing my sight of the hard realities of the sex-trade zones and gay neighborhoods with the vision of grace acting in the soul of the world to perceive creation and ultimately to save all human experience by affirming it as the experience of God.

In *tantra* yoga, the *kundalini* is mythologized as a sleeping serpent lying coiled about a sacred lingam in the first chakra. The yogic effort is to rouse the serpent to rise up through the spine to the seventh chakra, bringing ecstatic union with the divine. This cosmic energy that pours down from the sun making life possible is experienced also as the bioelectrical energy that courses through the body during sexual arousal. Orgasm is frequently mythologized as the release of small bursts of this energy.

"I sing the body electric," sang the graduating class of the New York High School for the Performing Arts in the 1981 film *Fame,* in their expectation of a vital, successful, and fulfilling life through which they'd achieve fame and, metaphorically, become one with the sun. "I sing the body electric," wrote Walt Whitman, in praise of his embodiment and his recognition of the body as the manifestation of spirit.

The teenagers of *Fame* were not a great deal different, though perhaps they'd had more opportunity to develop their talents, from the hustlers I met on the streets, looking for fame, a fulfilling life, and an escape from the pain of their childhood. They too, if not in the same words, looked forward to one day being one with the sun.

The nature mystic who sang the body electric and praised the self as the experience of God was not a great deal different, though he lived in a more innocent age, from the johns I interviewed. They too were seeking an expression of their love of beauty and an outlet for the pang they felt in seeing the vitality in the young people they courted on the streets.

And singing the body electric is not a great deal different from meditating on the flow of energy through the chakras.

Our bodies are powered through an intricate system of electrical and chemical exchanges which create a network of activity we know as conscious thought. Our sexuality is a direct experience of this energy. The same energy that patterns our thoughts and moves our bodies, impelling us to dance like the teenagers in *Fame* or to boogie like the kids on the meatracks, drives the lightning in the sky and radiates forth from the sun to give us warmth, light, and life. We are, indeed, one with the sun.

Working at the Tenderloin Clinic I'd been exposed to Reichian body-work as a form of psychotherapy. Dr. David Brandt, one of my supervisors, frequently emphasized the importance of observing a client's posture in doing diagnosis. A couple of years before I'd been in body-work therapy myself with Jeremy Naploha, a Reichian therapist.

According to the Reichians and neo-Reichians, the whole body is involved in psychological processes; consciousness and intelligence reside not merely in the brain. Similar to Adolphine's notion of blocks on the chakras, they suggest that traumas, fears, negative conditioning, and the like result in tightness and restriction in the body that distort both psychological and purely physiological processes. These can result not only in neurosis and mental illness, but also in psychosomatic disorders, cardiovascular disease, and perhaps even cancer.

Reichian therapy consists of practicing better and more complete releases of tension, through crying, screaming, vomiting, and coming to orgasm. Learning to allow spasmodic release and emotional catharsis helps prevent deformation of the nervous system. The surge of energy during orgasm can break the blocks and keep the system clear of restrictions to the vital flow. The role of orgasm in the human being then is more than just ejaculation or reception of genetic material. The aim of "total orgasm" is not simply to get narcissistic satisfaction, as suggested by many critics of the California-based fascination during the '70s with bigger and better orgasms, but to activate an important self-regulating mechanism in the mind-body system.

Orgasm is portrayed mythologically, as *kundalini* for instance, as a conscious experience of cosmic energy. Orgasm is certainly an experience of neurological dynamics. It has no content. Like a dream it is forgotten almost as soon as it is over.

Perhaps the function of sex and orgasm in human beings has been not only to clear the individual nervous system but—and consequently—to affect the way the nervous system itself has evolved. Human beings are sexually motivated differently from almost all other species on our planet. Because women's sexual interest is not restricted by an estrus cycle, human beings are sexually and psychologically available and motivated all the time. We engage in sexual foreplay beyond instinctual seduction rituals. We experience orgasm more completely, it appears, than other animals. And, at least among land animals, we alone have developed sophisticated language and complex brain functions. Perhaps our sexuality is in some ways responsible for, or at least intrinsic to, our evolution of intelligence and conscious thought.

In *The Myth of the Great Secret,* I noted that a problem with evolution by natural selection is that it doesn't really explain what standard is used for determining selection: it simply observes that survival results from survivability. I suggested that perhaps it was the ability to experience wonder, to feel curiosity, to develop myth, and to ask questions which force open the neural pathways that directed the path of survival up toward consciousness and humanity. Similarly, sexuality can be understood as the experience in the flesh of what in the mind is wonder and curiosity. Sexual attraction is the desire to know another's body, to feel the flesh, to experience the rhythms of the other's movement. It is the drive to enter into relationship with the other, to try to see from the other's perspective, and so to add complexity to one's own experience of life. And within the act of lovemaking itself, sex is the experience of joy in being embodied and of the body being caught up by a deeply primal, transpersonal force. It is not surprising that one consequence of such an experience of wonder should be genetic transfer and reproduction of life through time and through evolutionary advance. Sex as experience of the life force perhaps precedes sex as a tool for reproduction. Our sexuality, far from being a distraction from God, can be understood as the instrument by which God created us and continues to manifest himself to us.

Particularly in the sense that all of us are manifestations of the One Self, our experience of loving another person is our participation in the divine love for creation. And our experience of being loved is our perception of God's love for us. Indeed God has no way to demonstrate love for creatures except through the creatures' love for one another. This love for creation is not some curious will that creatures overcome their corporality. The flesh is the mode of creation. God's love for us and our love for God is experienced in our flesh.

We are blinded to the holiness of the flesh by fear and desire, by the tendency of the senses to get stuck, by our failure to see the whole, to see life in context, by our failure "to see the forest for the trees." But we will not develop vision by fleeing the flesh, by condemning our sexuality, by refusing to love God's manifestation in the flesh. A positive attitude toward sex can help bring us into touch with the resurrected body we carry, so unconsciously, along with us all our lives.

Isn't this positive attitude, this affirmation of incarnated human life, what is meant by the saviors' embrace of the human condition—even of sin and suffering? "God so loved the world. . . ."

The task of the mythic hero is to discover the mystical truth of his own essence and to see that that essence is also the essence of the world. Thus, through having saved himself by his magical journey through the Underworld and into the realm of the gods, he saves the world. The task of each of us is to discover the hero in ourselves, for the mythic hero is the symbol of the Self that is the essence of each one of us. And by that discovery we save the world.

The world and the flesh have familiarly been posed as the enemies of the spiritual life. People have been urged to flee the world and conquer the flesh. But these are not so much enemies to be vanquished as obstacles to be overcome and transformed. If we want to be heroes, especially in modern, psychologically sophisticated times when we understand the nature of myth and symbol, we must save the world and the flesh, not abandon them.

TWELVE

The Saviors
of the World

The wisdom of saving the world and the flesh is told around the world in myth, fairy tale, and religion. We sometimes find it in surprising places. In Joel Chandler Harris's story of Brer Rabbit and the Tar-baby, for instance, we find a classic description of the hero's confrontation with the world and a hint at the wisdom by which the hero saves himself and the world.

Brer Fox tried time and time again to catch Brer Rabbit, but time and time again Brer Rabbit got away. Then one day, Brer Fox got him some tar, and made himself a Tar-baby. Then he took this here Tar-baby and sat her in the road and then he lay off in the bushes. By-and-by along came Brer Rabbit—lippity, chippity, chippity, lippity—just as sassy as a jaybird.

Brer Fox, he lay low.

This story of Brer Rabbit parallels an Indian folk story of the Buddha. Long before he was incarnated as the wise teacher who would enter nirvana in his lifetime, his spirit lived as an heroic, young adventurer called Prince Five-weapons. On the journey back to his father's kingdom, following completion of his martial training, he came to a dark and forbidding forest in which lived a fierce ogre called Sticky Hair. He was warned to go another way, but he was confident and fearless and set forth straight into the ogre's domain.

Brer Rabbit's confrontation with the Tar-baby was a little less intentional, but soon no less militant. For when the Tar-baby did not respond to his salutation, even after hollerin', in case the Tar-baby was deaf, Brer Rabbit took it upon himself to teach the Tar-baby a lesson in civility. So he threatened to whack her up side the head if she didn't take off her hat and say howdy.

Brer Fox, he lay low, and the Tar-baby just stayed still, saying nothing. Brer Rabbit drew back his fist and took her a whack on the side of the head. His fist went right into the tar and stuck there. After threatening to hit her again if she didn't let him loose, Brer Rabbit fetched her a whack with his other hand. And that stuck too.

Brer Rabbit kicked the Tar-baby with first one foot, then the other, and finally, in desperation, butted her with his head 'til he was stuck firm to the Tar-baby in five places. Just then Brer Fox sauntered forth from his hiding place and, just as innocent as a mockingbird, greeted Brer Rabbit. This time it was Brer Rabbit that ain't sayin' nothing. Well, Brer Fox was pretty pleased with himself. He'd caught Brer Rabbit fair and square. Ain't nobody made Brer Rabbit try to strike up an acquaintance with the Tar-baby. And nobody invited him to stick his hands, his feet, or his head in the tar. He did that all on his own. And now he'd be stuck 'til Brer Fox went and lit a brush fire, pulled him out of the tar, and barbecued him for lunch.

Brer Rabbit saw he'd been caught dead to rights and he talked mighty humble. "I don't care what you do with me, Brer Fox, so long as you don't fling me in that there briar patch."

Seeing as how it was going to be a lot of work to make a fire and apparently not caring whether lunch was cooked or raw, Brer Fox reckoned he could just hang the rabbit.

"Hang me just as high as you please, Brer Fox, but for the Lawd's sake, don't fling me in that briar patch," said Brer Rabbit.

Seeing as how he had no rope, Brer Fox decided to drown the rabbit.

"Drown me just as deep as you please, Brer Fox, but don't fling me in that briar patch," said Brer Rabbit.

Seeing as how there was no water around, the Fox said he'd just skin the rabbit.

"Skin me, Brer Fox, snatch out my eyeballs, pull out my hair, tear out my ears by the roots and cut off my legs," said Brer Rabbit, "but please, please, Brer Fox, don't fling me in the briar patch."

Well, Brer Fox was pretty fed up with Brer Rabbit's whining. He really didn't care about eating him so much as he did hurting him as bad as he could. So he caught him up by the hind legs, pulled him out of the Tar-baby, slung him around in the air, and flung him right into the middle of that there briar patch.

There was a considerable flutter where the rabbit struck and Brer Fox hung around to see what was going to happen. By and by he heard someone calling to him, and way up the hill he saw Brer Rabbit sitting on a log combing the tar out of his fur.

"Bred and born in the briar patch, Brer Fox, bred and born in the briar patch. Briars can't hurt me," sang Brer Rabbit as he skipped off just as lively as a cricket in the embers.

To become a hero, the Buddha had to overcome fear and trick death. When he was seated beneath the Bo Tree on the Immovable Spot, where he would soon attain his enlightenment, he was assailed by Kama-Mara, the Lord of Desire and Death. To put an end to the temptation he touched his hand to the earth, proclaiming his right to be there. And the earth mother-goddess roared in a voice of thunder that terrified Kama-Mara and all his minions, so that they fled, leaving the Buddha in peace. He had seen that so long as he "stayed grounded," firm in his resolve, unfrightened by the illusions of fear and desire, he was unstuck.

But the confrontation with Kama-Mara over the right to be on the Immovable Spot was not to come for many incarnations after Prince Five-weapons' battle with Sticky Hair. He had another adventure to deal with first.

The Prince took his name from the five weapons he bore: poisoned arrows, sword, spear, and club, and his own body trained in martial arts. With these he expected to slay the ogre who, in turn, took his name, as one might imagine, from the thick hair all over his body into which stuck any weapon used against him.

Five-weapons, upon finding the ogre, smote him with his arrows. They stuck in the hair. Then he tried his fabulous sword. It too stuck. One by one the weapons, including, of course, the Prince's hands, feet, and head, got stuck fast in the ogre's hair. But the Prince was undaunted.

Hesitating before eating him up, the ogre asked the youth, "Why are you not afraid?"

"Why should I be afraid? Death is certain in every life," declared the Prince. "Besides I carry in my belly a thunderbolt for a weapon you cannot withstand. If you eat me up, the thunderbolt will blow you to pieces. And, in that case, we'll both perish."

Sticky Hair, not quite as difficult to convince, but just as credulous as Brer Fox, submitted to the wisdom of the Future Buddha, was converted, practiced self-denial, and became a divine spirit dwelling in the forest.

Each of us is equipped with five weapons. For, as Campbell points out (following A. K. Coomaraswamy and others), the five weapons are the five external senses with which we contact the world. Sticky Hair and the Tar-baby represent that world. In his enlightenment the Buddha discovered that the world that threatens to eat us up, tear out our ears by the roots, and cut off our legs is but the physical manifestation of our thoughts and experiences, like a dream or mirage. But when we engage the world through our senses we become stuck in it. We take it seriously. We become imprisoned in our own creation, caught in the form we give to our experience of self, valuing one thing over another, succumbing to fear and desire, resisting life. We get stuck in the world because we fail to look beyond it, understand it in a greater context, or take responsibility for our participation in its creation.

The hero is wiser than the world. Oh, Brer Rabbit had got himself stuck all right, but when he saw the nature of the Tar-baby and the grinning face of Brer Fox, he very quickly got wise.

What he knew—that Brer Fox didn't—is that rabbits are different from foxes: that people live in different universes with different assumptions, expectations, aims, and values based on their upbringing and experience. Because the fox was so full of hate and lived in such a one-dimensional world, he assumed because he himself wouldn't want to fall into a briar patch Brer Rabbit was telling the truth when he pleaded with him not to throw him into them there briars. The fox fell for the ruse and the hero got away.

Young Five-weapons revealed to Sticky Hair that besides the physical world in which swords cut and clubs crush and mangle, there is an etheric world in which Sticky Hair's defenses could not protect him. In Indian thought, there were not five senses but six, for mind was considered a sense. It was through the power of mind to observe the other senses and to discover the wisdom that death need not be feared, that the Prince was armed with the lightning bolt.*

*This bolt, by the way, is the power that transforms Billy Batson into Captain Marvel in the modern children's myth. Invocation of the mantra "Shazam" (an acronym for the heroic qualities of Solomon's wisdom, Hercules' strength, Atlas' stamina, Zeus' power, Achilles' courage, and Mercury's speed) reminds the hero trapped in the illusion of human personality of who he really is and releases super powers.

If even comic books and Saturday morning TV reveal the essential wisdom, why do we fail to possess the powers? The Buddha answered that, of course, we do possess them: Behold the universe we have created. But we are so mesmerized by that creation that we do not remember our ego-transcendent identity and we do not realize that we are creating it just the way we want to.

Another comic-book-style myth also answers that question. In the 1981 TV show *The Greatest American Hero* Ralph Hinckley, a well-motivated if feckless high school teacher, possesses super powers when he dons a suit given him by benevolent extra-terrestrials. But he can only use the powers ineptly because he has lost the instruction book that came with the suit. We all have lost the instructions (hidden within the myths). We have all forgotten that we were born into the world wearing Ralph's supersuit. And so the world appears greedy, lustful, and angry.

Our modern vantage point allows us to observe ourselves (though it is precisely this ability which is responsible for our loss of belief). We are conscious of the operation of our minds. Just as our minds are responsible for the advances we have achieved, so are they for the problems that have resulted. And yet only our ability to observe ourselves can solve these problems which, like Tar-baby and Sticky Hair, seem to trap us more deeply the more we grapple with them. Only a change in consciousness, in how we perceive the world, can save us from being trapped in it.

The wisdom of the mythological teachings is always, in part, concerned with how to get unstuck from the world, how to see with the spiritual eye beyond the senses to who we really are. This wisdom is what is conveyed in the stories of the heroes' journeys, for the heroes are always seeking their true identity.

The heroes of Mahayana Buddhism are Siddhartha Gautama, who entered nirvana and became the Lord Buddha, and the Bodhisattva Avalokitesvara, who renounced nirvana to save all sentient beings. Compared to early Buddhism, which taught that life was all suffering and that each individual had to work to escape from life into a nirvana that was simply extinction, the Mahayana, a reinterpretation of the Buddha's teachings several hundred years after his death, was relatively life-affirming.

The Mahayana sages taught that the world arises through a process of "mutual coorigination" in which nothing is known individually or independently but only relatively in its interacting with everything else in a great cosmic unity. Since nothing is absolute, nothing can be known of absolute truth. All knowledge is empty. Even the teachings of the Buddha are not absolute, but only hints at a greater, unknowable, ineffable truth. The denial of all absolute distinctions implies that there is no ascertainable difference between samsara, the world of change and apparent suffering, and nirvana, the state beyond change and suffering. *Samsara* is *nirvana.* The world is no different from heaven. They taught a radical monism in which all beings are manifestations of the One Being. The illusion from which all must be saved is that individual existence is real. The Mahayanists recommended compassion for others as the "skillful means" of attaining enlightenment and escaping rebirth. They accepted life in the world, not just in the monastery, as an exercise in gaining enlightenment.

To communicate the emptiness of absolute truth, radical monism, and compassion as the means to salvation, the Mahayanists told the story of the Bodhisattva Avalokitesvara. This young saint, whose name means "The Lord looking down in pity," had striven through many incarnations to enter nirvana. But in the last stages of his enlightenment Avalokitesvara saw that since individual existence was illusory and he was not separate from other beings, it made no sense to flee life into nirvana. Indeed, it was not really possible: if all are one, then each can be saved only when all are saved. Avalokitesvara was swept by a wave of compassion for all beings. He renounced escape from the wheel of samsara. He chose to remain in the world, to be incarnated again and again through lifetimes without number, in order to assist all sentient beings to achieve release. It would not be right, he thought, to flee the world, and leave others behind to suffer.

Indeed, seeing that it was better for one to suffer rather than all, he agreed to take upon himself all the suffering of the world. And he willed that the merit for this selfless act should go out from him to all beings, so that all should be saved. I will not enter nirvana, he vowed, until all beings have entered nirvana.

The Bodhisattva's vow is expressed ritually in a litany all Mahayanists are urged to repeat:

However innumerable beings are, I vow to save them;
however inexhaustible the passions are, I vow to extinguish
them;

172 In Search of God in the Sexual Underworld

*however immeasurable the Dharmas are, I vow to master
them;*
however incomparable the Buddha-truth is, I vow to attain it. *

In the Japanese story of the bodhisattva Amida there is a
curious variation on Avalokitesvara's vow. As Amida was about
to enter nirvana, he too felt compassion for all beings. He declared that he would not complete his entry into nirvana unless
it were guaranteed that all beings who had called upon his help,
saying his name as few as ten times in their lives, would at death
gain immediate admission to the Pure Land. He subsequently
entered nirvana, becoming Amida, the Sun Buddha. To followers
of Shin Buddhism, called the Pure Land Sect, his departure was
a sure sign that salvation awaits those who honor the name of
Amida and reverently chant his mantra: *Namo Amida Butsu*
(Honor to the Buddha Amida). Perhaps soon after dawn on
August 6, 1945, when citizens of Hiroshima observed the noon-
day sun descending upon them several hours early, some of them
saw not the wrath of America annihilating them in an act of war,
but the face of Amida the Sun Buddha welcoming them into the
Pure Land, making them one with the sun.

Avalokitesvara is portrayed as bisexual, both male and female,
uniting the opposites. In this androgyny he personifies the principle of emptiness: *samsara* is *nirvana, nirvana* is *samsara:* there
are no exclusive categories. Today bisexual has also come to
mean being both heterosexual and homosexual, uniting the opposites.
    When I first learned about Avalokitesvara, I was not worldly

*Readers of J.D. Salinger's stories may recall that Seymour and Buddy taught
their younger siblings to recite the Great Vows as a blessing before meals. While
at a business luncheon, Zooey Glass once tried to break the habit of muttering
the sequence under his breath. For his effort, during the meal, he choked on
a cherrystone clam.

enough to distinguish between these two meanings of bisexual. Learning of bisexual gods (of which Avalokitesvara is but one in a crowded pantheon) forced me to reevaluate deeply ingrained prejudices about homosexuality. For the myths tell us that from the mystical perspective the distinctions between male and female and between homosexual and heterosexual—as between time and eternity, pluralism and monism—are meaningless.

Even Saint Paul declared that in Christ there is neither male nor female. And the Jesus of the Gnostic Gospel of Thomas declared that until one had made the male as female and the female as male, one could not enter the kingdom. Like the myth of the androgynous bodhisattva, this suggests that one has to overcome the tendency of the mind to differentiate and value before one can perceive the unity of life. For what Jesus called the Kingdom was probably not an afterlife, but a mystical realization of the ultimate unity of all beings. In the canonical, but only slightly less gnostic, Gospel of John, Jesus prayed that all may be one, even as he had realized he was one with the Father. In Buddhist terms, Jesus was a bodhisattva, for he took upon himself the sin—the pain, the brokenness, the blindness, the stupidity and apparent failure—of the world.

Jesus—a world savior like the Buddha or the Bodhisattva and a battler with the world and its suffering like Brer Rabbit and Prince Five-weapons—discovered that the way to overcome the world and the flesh was to embrace it, the way to overcome death was to die. Jesus was nailed to a cross. The cross, extending in the four directions of the compass, represented the world. Jesus suffered five wounds by which his senses were crucified on the tree of the knowledge of good and evil. The fruit of that tree, when eaten by Adam, resulted in the vision of the polarities which trapped him and all his offspring in the world of suffering. Crucifixion on that tree resulted for Jesus in the vision beyond the polarities.

The story of the confirmation to Thomas the Apostle, who said he would not believe in Jesus' return until he had placed his own hands in Jesus' wounds, is the only indication in Scripture that Jesus had been *nailed* to his cross. Elsewhere it is simply reported he was crucified. As almost every depiction of the scene shows of the two thieves, victims of crucifixion were ordinarily tied by the arms to a horizontal beam and left to die, usually of asphixiation when the weight of the hanging body causes the muscles in the chest and diaphragm to go into spasm.

But Jesus is said to have suffered five wounds: in the hands and feet, caused by nails with which he was affixed to the cross, and in the heart, caused by a spear with which he was stabbed by the Roman Centurion, who seems to have been a believer, to make certain he was dead (and, incidentally, to drain the blood from his body as required in the preparation of the Passover lamb). The crucifixion was cut short and the men killed because it was necessary to dispose of their bodies. The feast of Passover was beginning and Jews would be forbidden to prepare graves.

The five wounds were significant of the opening of the senses by which the vision of the Kingdom could be regained. Five "wounds" appear similarly on the body of Tara, the goddess of compassion, born of a tear of the Bodhisattva Avalokitesvara. She bears openings in her hands and feet and in her forehead; from within Tara's "wounds" eyes look out to see the mystically transformed world.*

---

*On page 109 in *The Time Falling Bodies Take to Light,* William Irwin Thompson observes:

The slit of the vulva appears like a wound made by a spear, and so the spear becomes a phallus. But the vulva is the magical wound that bleeds and heals itself every month, and because it bleeds in sympathy with the dark of the moon, the vulva is an expression not of physiology but of cosmology. The moon dies and is reborn; woman bleeds but does not die, and when she does not bleed for ten lunar months, she brings forth new life. It is easy to see how Paleolithic man would be in awe of woman, and how woman's mysteries would be at the base of a religious cosmology. We can see just how long-lived such iconology is if we stop to remember the spear that makes the wound in Christ's side, and recall just how many medieval paintings pictured Christ exposing his wound.

On the cross, Jesus said, at least partially in the ritual language of Hebrew, words that have perplexed many Christians: *Eli, eli, lema sabacthani.* And (according to the two Gospels that record this story) he then gave up his spirit to God. These are the opening words of Psalm 22, a prayer that is part of a cycle of texts that refer to the "Suffering Servant," the Just Man who, though innocent, takes upon himself the sins of the people, becoming the scapegoat to suffer for them, once for all. Jesus' intonation of the words, "My God, my God, why have you forsaken me?" was not a sign of his despair. It was very truly his recitation of what in a different context we know as the Bodhisattva's vow.

By the merit of his act he became more than just a man trapped in space and time. He became, as he prayed in the Priestly Prayer in the Saint John Gospel, one with all humanity. And he was crowned, with a crown of thorns and briars, King of the Universe, Savior of the World.

To Dismas, the Good Thief, Jesus declared: "This day you are with me in Paradise." The word in Scripture is Paradise, not heaven; it was the word for the Garden in Genesis. Jesus seems to have been declaring not that Dismas would enter some ethereal afterlife, but that, because he had recognized he was responsible for his own acts and deserved crucifixion and, unlike the other thief, did not taunt Jesus to free him, Dismas' cross had also become the tree of life and to him also was restored the vision of the Garden.

Jesus' words to Dismas that the willingness to accept responsibility for one's own acts restored one to Paradise, and Jesus' own willingness to go beyond that to accept responsibility for the acts

---

The labial wound in the side of Christ is an expression that the male shaman, to have magical power, must take on the power of woman. The wound that does not kill Christ is the magical labial wound; it is the seal of the resurrection and an expression of the myth of eternal recurrence. From Christ to the Fisher King of the Grail legends, the man suffering from a magical wound is no ordinary man; he is the man who has transcended the duality of sexuality, the man with a vulva, the shamanistic androgyne.

of the whole world, reveal an essential meaning of the myth of the crucifixion. The Christian message, similar to yet differently inflected from the Buddhist, is at least on one level that, while the suffering of the world may not be escaped, it can be transcended. In the Gnostic Acts of John, leading the Apostles in a kind of mystic dance, Jesus instructed them: "Learn how to suffer and you shall be able not to suffer." And that is accomplished by taking responsibility for the world in all its manifestations, by embracing it in oneself and in others as the means by which the senses can be opened, by accepting things just as they are without resistance, by practicing compassion not condemnation. This is more consistent with Jesus' practical admonitions to forgive sinners and love even one's enemies than with the later tendency of Christians to judge righteously as sinful certain lifestyles and to persecute those who did not adhere to a rigid standard of orthodoxy.

Jesus, unlike many of his followers, saw what Brer Rabbit saw: different people live in different universes and one person's briar patch is another's home; one person's hell is another's heaven; and to be one with the Ultimate, to be one with God, one has to embrace all the heavens and all the hells equally. And so from his perspective as the Christ—the ultimate Self—he was willing to fling himself into the briars. For the road of adventure, the road back to the Garden, leads right into the middle of the briar patch. The briars of Brer Rabbit's escape and the briars of Jesus' crown, and, incidentally, the briars of my Advent eagle's nest, are one and the same: the occasion to change the way we look at the world.

"In a twinkle we shall all be changed," said Saint Paul.

Not in a twinkle, but in the agony of three hours on the cross and the emptiness of three days in the tomb, Jesus Christ was changed from man to god. His body was transformed, the myth tells, from a body of flesh, which, trapped in individuality by the perspective of the senses, could suffer and die, to a body of light and glory, which, freed from the limitations of perspective, could pass through walls and cover distance in an instant.

The Resurrection is considered the central mystery of Christianity. In it are clues for how to live in the world and in the flesh. That is what the mystery is about. Too frequently, however, the Resurrection is presented not about life in the flesh, but about some sort of disembodied afterlife.

Just as the bodhisattva, in one version of the vow, offers himself as "the food and drink in the famine of the ages' end," so Jesus said his physical body would be meat and his blood drink for his followers so they could enter his Kingdom. He offered himself as the lamb of the Passover sacrifice. The blood of this lamb, smeared on the doorposts, alerted the Angel of Death to pass over the homes of the Chosen People; its flesh fed them during their pilgrimage to the Promised Land, the Pure Land. And of his body that would be sacrificed, Jesus said, "If you destroy this temple, I shall build it up again in three days."

The disciples perhaps took his metaphor of reconstruction too literally—an error they made often. They consistently misunderstood his message, expecting in the Kingdom not mystical vision but political accession. And so it was that on the third day after Jesus' death, when they went to the place where his remains had been laid, to their dismay they found only an empty tomb, not a reconstituted Jesus. It must have seemed to them that their Lord had failed to rebuild the temple that had been destroyed or resurrect the victim who had been ritually sacrificed for the new Passover.

But then one by one they began to experience strange events. At unexpected times they felt Jesus' presence. In the gardener on Joseph Arimathea's land, Mary recognized him. In a stranger two of the disciples met on the way to the little town of Emmaus outside Jerusalem, when they sat down to eat together, they experienced him. In a shadowy figure cooking breakfast over a fire by the edge of the sea, to which as sailors they'd returned after Jesus' death, they recognized him. In the upper room in which they'd hidden in fear, the Apostles saw him in a mystical body.

John Dominic Crossan, a Biblical theologian under whom I studied in Chicago, argued that the notable differences between the narratives in the four Gospels suggest that the simple physical resuscitation of Jesus was not the real sense of the Resurrection intended by the Evangelists. If, as so many have maintained afterwards, the historicity of such a resuscitation were the central fact of Christianity upon which all else rises or falls, Crossan argued, the accounts should agree in their report of the historical events. After all, the essence of historicity *is* consistency among witnesses' accounts. But the accounts are not consistent: the Evangelists treated the Resurrection just as they did other events in Jesus' life—not as historical facts—but as symbolic carriers of spiritual and mystical meaning. What the Gospels do agree on is that on the third day the tomb was empty and soon afterwards the disciples experienced mystical phenomena that are variously depicted as apparitions of Jesus, their ability to work wonders, and the descent of the Holy Spirit.

What actually happened to Jesus' body remains a mystery. Perhaps the corpse was reanimated, as most Christians believe. Perhaps it was stolen, as suggested in the Matthew Gospel, by entrepreneurs, hoping it might still possess some healing power or at least bring a small fee from pilgrims. Perhaps it simply disappeared.*

Or perhaps the disciples literally consumed the body of Jesus. After all, at the Last Supper Jesus had taken bread and blessed it and given it to his disciples, showing them "This is my body" and instructing them "take and eat." And he had taken a cup of wine and blessed it and given it to them, showing them also "This

---

*Recent evidence from the mysterious shroud of Turin suggests that the body emitted, or perhaps turned into, light or some form of scorching radiation. The bodies of yogis have occasionally been reported to dissolve into light or flame at their deaths.

is the cup of my blood, take and drink." Thus he would be physically present in the disciples' own bodies.

What the Resurrection seems to indicate is that Christ has remained mystically, yet also physically, present. This is, of course, what is meant by the sacrament of the Eucharist. For two millennia the Roman Church has insisted that the eucharistic bread and wine are not merely symbols but are in fact, transsubstantially, the body and blood of Jesus. The revulsion we feel when we consider the cannibalism inherent in this image or in Jesus' straightforward instructions at the Last Supper only reveals how little we appreciate sacramentality or understand the meaning of the historicity of the Incarnation. For the historicity of Christianity is itself mythological. The myth of historicity means that spiritual reality is embodied in time and in the flesh.

In the ancient Roman liturgy of the Easter Vigil, grains of incense were enfixed with stylized wax nails into the five cardinal points of a cross inscribed on the Paschal Candle. The candle represented Christ as the "light of the world." The grains of incense represented the sweetness of the wounds by which the world was transformed. To the right and left of the cross were inscribed the numerals for the current year; above and below, the letters Alpha and Omega: the cross, which is the acceptance of things just as they are, is formed by the intersection of the temporal and the eternal.

With consciously sexual symbolism recognized by the Church, the priest who prepared the Paschal Candle then plunged it three times, each time deeper, into a pool of water. As he did this, he prayed that the Spirit descend into the water—which, representing the material world transformed, would be used throughout the coming year for baptism—making it fruitful for regeneration so that those who partook of its sacrament would be "born again new children in true innocence."

This ceremony manifests the tradition that Jesus' death fecundated a new earth. This image, in turn, manifests the even older tradition of the slaughtered king or corn god, who sacrificed himself at the end of his reign in order to bring life to the soil upon which his people depended for food.

Some years ago I wandered into the chapel of the Catholic ministry at the University of California at Santa Barbara. Behind the altar hung a huge mural of the crucifixion in stark black and white, like a photo collage. I was stunned by it. The corpus was surrounded by chromosomal and genetic structures on one side and interplanetary and galactic images on the other. Jesus' body was formed of vascular and striated muscle tissue. It stood before and grew into a cross that was a stylization of the female reproductive organs. The arms of the cross were like fallopian tubes. Within an ovarian form on the left crossarm, a skeletal fetus reached out its hand to insert its fingers into the print of the nail in the savior's palm. Above Jesus' face, bowed in life-bestowing death, the spectral hands of the Father blessing his Son formed the head of the phallus by which the Christ was fructifying the material organic world. The painting, by Michael Dvortcsak, was titled in Teilhardian fashion: Christ Invests Himself Organically with the Very Majesty of His Universe.

The sacrifice of the incarnated Self accepting biological and mortal manifestation engenders new life in foetal humankind who reach out, like twin brother Thomas,* to test the validity of Resurrection. The blessed belief even of those who have not yet seen, but who have believed, transforms the nature of organic existence. Christ died not to enter into a new life by which he could escape the world, but to give us new life by which to

---

*In Gnostic Christianity, such as that presented in the non-canonical Gospel of Thomas, the image of the twin signified mystical identity with Jesus the Christ. The confirmation to Thomas signified the Apostle's realization that Jesus was flesh, and not a ghost, in Thomas' own body.

experience that world, in the very flesh in which the Christ/Self remains forever incarnate.

In promising to "master the immeasurable dharmas," the Bodhisattva Avalokitesvara identified himself with all beings. In realizing the radical oneness of all consciousness, he became the One Being incarnated in all, the one able to perceive the world from all possible perspectives. Hence Avalokitesvara became savior of the world because he is the only being in the world and he has saved himself, and everyone else, by his realization that none are saved till all are saved, and by his choice to save himself by saving all of us—the ultimate act of enlightened, radical self-interest.

Joseph Campbell writes of the Bodhisattva:

Peace is at the heart of all because Avalokitesvara-Kwannon, the mighty Bodhisattva, Boundless Love, includes, regards, and dwells within (without exception) every sentient being. The perfection of the delicate wings of an insect, broken in the passage of time, he regards—and he himself is both their perfection and their disintegration. The perennial agony of man, self-torturing, deluded, tangled in the net of his own tenuous delirium, frustrated, yet having within himself, undiscovered, absolutely unutilized, the secret of release: this too he regards—and is. Serene above man, the angels; below man, the demons and unhappy dead: these all are drawn to the Bodhisattva by the rays of his jewel hands, and they are he, as he is they. The bounded, shackled centers of consciousness, myriadfold, on every plane of existence (not only in this present universe, limited by the Milky Way, but beyond, into the reaches of space), galaxy beyond galaxy, world beyond world of universes, coming into being out of the timeless pool of the void, bursting into life, and like a bubble therewith vanishing: time and time again: lives by the multitude: all suffering: each bounded in the tenuous, tight circle of itself—lashing, killing, hating, and desiring peace beyond victory: these are all the children, the mad figures of the transitory yet inexhaustible, long world dream of the All-Regarding, whose essence is the essence of Emptiness: "The Lord Looking Down in Pity."

But the name means also: "The Lord Who is Seen Within." We are all reflexes of the image of the Bodhisattva. The sufferer within us is that divine being. We and that protecting father are one. This is the redeeming insight. And so it must be known that, though this ignorant, limited, self-defending, suffering body may regard itself as threatened by some other —the enemy—that one too is the God. . . . we live not in this physique only, but in all bodies, all physiques of the world, as the Bodhisattva. (*The Hero with a Thousand Faces,* pages 160–62)

That is why all Mahayanists ritually recite the vows (and why Zooey Glass choked on a clam for failing to do so). To forget the vows is to forget one's own truest identity and miss the ultimate redeeming insight.

Jesus' mystical vision had shown him that his individuality too was evanescent. He had seen that in the destruction of his body, sacrificed and devoured, surrendering form back into emptiness —as ego consciousness surrenders to unconsciousness—he would be transformed: he would dissolve back into the collective. In being subsumed he would become one with his followers, incorporated into them, seeing through their eyes, hearing with their ears, touching them with their hands—free of individual perspective.

In entering death, proclaiming the bodhisattva/savior's vow to suffer for us all, Jesus is reborn in each person. He has become one with the consciousness that perceives all experience and founds all existence. Each of us is Jesus reborn—not so much, of course, in our bodies of matter (born of mother) which exist in different places in space and time from the body of Jesus—but in our pure awareness (born of virgin) of life simply as it is in the present moment. In Christ (that is, in the pure awareness that is the consciousness in each of us) we all rise from the dead, for we are reborn in children over and over again, not necessarily as reincarnating individuals but as the life itself that causes our children to grow into adults and then to die to make space for more children and more life.

The myth of the Resurrection gives physical reality to Jesus' spiritual discovery of life beyond death—not simply of continuous living, but of an abundant, transpersonal vitality beyond space and time. The Resurrection reveals how rooted is the temporal in the eternal, the individual in the collective, and the physical in the spiritual.

The myth of the resurrection of the body (Jesus' in history and ours at the Second Coming) signifies that life keeps coming back in the flesh. To see that is to see that death need not be feared, that embodied life is good, that we are all manifestations of the same life. To see that is to be born again of the water (of the ocean out of which life first grew and of the amniotic water of our birth) and of the spirit (which is the breath respiring through all of us, and which, as William James saw, is modulated into consciousness in each of us). It is to see that we are all risen from the dead because of God's act of creation of space and time.

In time the creative will is our experience of tense. For the future into which we are being born is always being created in time out of the past from which we have been reborn. Indeed, being reborn means seeing that we are that creative will knowing itself and choosing out of infinite compassion and interest to be all beings.

In space that will is seen as light. For all life grows up from the earth driven by the power pouring down from the sun. In his resurrection Jesus became light, one with the sun. Thus the bread and the wine really *are* the body and blood of Jesus because the wheat growing out of rich soil, nourished by the deterioration of organic matter in the dark humus, is the embodiment of the light, and the wine, pressed from the grapes, invigorated by the propagation of yeasts in the rich red juices, is the blood of the sun

The point of sacrament is to give physical reality to spiritual truth. Jesus' conquest of death is his presence in the flesh of his followers. And the point of transforming our vision is to find in the flesh, with all its sexual immediacy, the sacrament of our experience of God. True innocence, Christ invested organically, a new way to see the world, vision transformed, the fecundation of a new heaven and a new earth—this is what the spiritual teachings promise. Such vision will, in fact, transform the world of history. That is what the Second Coming refers to: when our sights have all changed we will see that Christ comes again because, of course, he's never left. Like Avalokitesvara he has remained in our bodies as us.

THIRTEEN

Seeing with Different Eyes

The 17th-century European poet-mystic Johannes Scheffler, who wrote under the name Angelus Silesius, asked:

> *Who is God? No one can tell*
> *He is not dark of night*
> *nor light of day*
> *He is not One nor Many*
> *nor a Father as some say.*
> *Nor is he wisdom,*
> *intellect, or even mercy;*
> *He is not Being—*
> *nor non-Being*
> *neither thing*
> *nor no-thing.*
> *Perhaps He is*
> *what I and all*
> *who ever did or will have being*
> *could ever be capable of seeing*
> *before becoming what He is.*

Or again:

> *It is as if God played a game*
> *immersed in contemplation;*
> *and from this game*
> *all worlds arose*
> *in endless variation.*
> (*The Book of Angelus Silesius,* tr. Frederick Franck)

The primary religious intuition, the "perennial philosophy," found with various inflections throughout human culture, is that the world comes into existence in the experience of the multitude of sentient beings, all of which arise through a process of mutual creation from some underlying stratum of reality that always, and necessarily, eludes specification. This fundamental reality is hidden by the forms in which it manifests. We are blind to it even though we see it everywhere. The mystics, prophets, and visionaries have told us that the new way to see the world—the way to save the world—is to see the universal substrate shining forth behind the forms.

This substrate is called God. And God is the ground of all acts of knowing. Yet, because knowledge requires a vantage point and there is nothing outside God in relation to which he might know himself, as Meister Eckhart observes, God cannot know his own being. It is God's inability to know himself—that is, the freedom from the limitations of a perspective enjoyed by the Divine—that is the core of the mystical notions, so familiar in Zen Buddhism but pervasive throughout the mystical world, of unknowing, of emptiness, and of the Void. In order to know himself this God must assume perspectives. From the One must come the Many, so that the many can know each other as the One. Thus Mohammed said of God, "I was a hidden treasure and I loved to be known, so I created the world that I might be known."

God individuates in order to know himself as the universe. We are God's sense organs. The accumulation of all possible experiences from all possible perspectives constitutes God's experience of self. This is the redeeming insight. As Scheffler wrote:

> *He is enlightened,*
> *liberated.*
> *Who sees all things as One—*
> *unseparated.*

Thus, because what "ego" means is just one's perspective, this insight calls us to overcome selfishness and egotism; it demands justice and equity and inspires compassion.

Beyond our location in space and our location in time (which is our history) there is nothing to us. We are the sum of our experiences; no ego other than the perspective that the experience of space and time provides us. To recognize that we are but perspectives of the Divine faculty of knowing calls us beyond our egos by calling us to be gods. And this is what self-actualization means: that we remain true to our experience and manifest ourselves as gods. That is why actualization is something for each of us to strive for. And that is why when Toby Marotta began to talk to me of how the countercultural call for self-actualization and respect for others' difference had brought about a "revolution through consciousness change" in homosexual men and women, I heard not only the researching social scientist, but also the Guardian Angel.

What Toby talked about as sociological and political phenomena resonated with what I'd come to know as a moral and mystical reality: that society will work best for everyone when each person works to realize his or her own potential. This is the liberationist and libertarian argument that a world of individuals consciously seeking their own informed self-interest will result in a peaceful and harmonious world with no real scarcities of goods or services. It is also the mystical revelation that all individuals are manifestations of a divine reality that in each seeks to experience the wholeness of creation and that holds, despite appearance sometimes to the contrary, good intention for the whole world and a loving, positive regard for each individual.

The realization that in God we are all One—unseparated, that I am "the others" (though from my perspective, when I experience being the others, they seem "out there" and I seem "in here") is what informs the liberationist-libertarian self-interest.

My own self-interest requires that I live in harmony and sharing with all other beings, for unless I am compassionate and sharing I will not receive from them the goods, services, concern, and assistance I need to fulfill my own self-interest. That self-interest becomes merely self-absorption and narcissism when the informed vision of the world it demands fails to be radical enough. Clinging to my perspective and resisting the others' efforts to make me part of their experience, not choosing to be open and honest with them, shuts me off from the unity that would give my life meaning and transform my world.

The decision to self-actualize calls me to enlist the assistance of all others around me by assisting them in their actualization. Radical self-interest, in the words of the counterculture and according to Toby Marotta's explanation of liberationist political activity, demands and produces a revolution through consciousness change.

Jesus said the Kingdom of God does not come by expectation; it will not be here or there, for the Kingdom is spread across the earth and people do not see it. The Kingdom of God is within you. To discover the Kingdom we must change the way we see the world and the flesh. We must change ourselves. That, of course, is precisely what is accomplished by the hero's journey. Of that accomplishment, Campbell says:

> The aim is not to *see,* but to realize that one *is,* that essence; then one is free to wander as that essence in the world. Furthermore: the world too is of that essence. The essence of oneself and the essence of the world: these two are one. Hence separateness, withdrawal, is no longer necessary. Wherever the hero may wander, whatever he may do, he is ever in the presence of his own essence—for he has the perfected eye to see. (*The Hero with a Thousand Faces,* page 386)

The vision of the unity and goodness of the world is born in our own private and collective intention to transform the way we see things, to honor one another's struggle for self-actualization, interpreting it as an adjunct of our own. It calls us to affirm the choice of life-style of everyone, seeing, in each, God's decision to experience the world, even when that style seems as alien to ours as homosexuality or prostitution.

"For the world and time are the dance of the Lord in emptiness," wrote Thomas Merton:

> The silence of the spheres is the music of a wedding feast. The more we persist in misunderstanding the phenomena of life, the more we analyze them out into strange finalities and complex purposes of our own, the more we involve ourselves in sadness, absurdity, and despair. But it does not matter very much, because no despair of ours can alter the reality of things, or stain the joy of the cosmic dance which is always there.
>
> Yet the fact remains that we are invited to forget ourselves on purpose, cast our awful solemnity to the winds, and join in the general dance. (*New Seeds of Contemplation,* page 297)

For several years, I had regularly attended the Monday night meetings of San Francisco's Sufi Community. Worshipping with the Sufis was always uplifting and fun, mainly because the major practice of the worship was dance.

Sufism is the mystical tradition of Islam. Sufi Masters have developed a variety of practices to induce mystical states of consciousness. Jalaluddin Rumi, a thirteenth-century Persian Sufi and founder of the Mevlana Order, developed ritual dance. Because his dances consisted mostly of turning in place or spinning around a central point or pillar, Rumi's mendicant (in Persian, *darvish*) disciples came to be known in the West as "whirling dervishes."

Islam is a Western monotheistic religion. But because of geography it has always been more exposed than European Christianity to a plurality of religious beliefs. It is not surprising that

Sufism responded earlier to the birth of the modern age by developing pluralistic world religion offshoots. In the mid-nineteenth century in India, Sufi philosopher Hazrat Inayat Khan developed such a synthesis of religious ideas. Inayat Kahn's Sufism was brought to America as The Sufi Order of the West by his son, Pir Vilayat Kahn, and by an American disciple, Sam Lewis.

Obsessed with the mystical quest, Lewis, a San Francisco bohemian, had traveled to Japan to practice Zen and to India to study Sufism. In the early 1960s he returned to the United States an apostle with little idea of how to proceed. One day, while he was meditating in his little apartment on Clementina Street in San Francisco's South of Market district, he received an intuition to go to the Haight-Ashbury.

In those days the Haight was full of hippies playing in the streets, wandering around in LSD-induced trances. Some of them reported that as Sam Lewis walked down the street, he appeared surrounded by brilliant light. The hippies would follow him, like a Pied Piper, to Golden Gate Park, where he taught Sufi chants and later the dance practices that came to him in his meditations. The dances were simple rhythmic repetitive circle dances, like those taught kindergarten children.

Soon Lewis developed a regular following. He moved to a house on Precita Avenue in the Bernal Heights district to make room for a community of students. Though he died in 1971, after only three years of teaching, his Sufi community grew strong and continued to hold meetings to perform the dances in San Francisco, Berkeley, and Marin County.

Sufism of the West has spread all over the United States. When the hippies left San Francisco as that phase of the counterculture ended, those who'd been affected by Sam Lewis took the dances with them back to their hometowns or country communes. After my own departure from San Francisco to the Smoky Mountains, I found a thriving community of Sufis outside Asheville, North Carolina, still performing the dances.

The symbol of the Sufis is a winged heart. Sufism, its Masters

say, is not a way of the head but of the heart. The way to fly to
God is to open the heart, to be human and to love and offer life
in service to God and to others. The primary mystical teaching
of Sufism is contained in the Sufi interpretation of the Islamic
credo *La Ilaha El Allah Hu.* What most Moslems interpret as
a declaration of monotheism, "There is no God but Allah," the
Sufis understand as a revelation of ultimate unity: "There is no
reality but God." To remind themselves of the implications of
this, Sufis sometimes greet one another *Ya Azim:* "How wonder-
fully God manifests to me through you."

The present head of the San Francisco community is Wali Ali
Meyer, a Jewish Mississippian who had followed Lewis to the
park one day. Wali Ali usually conducted the Monday night
classes. He was no spaced-out guru and didn't look like a flower.
He was a big man with a bushy beard and hair pulled back into
a ponytail. He told jokes and made light of himself. Sometimes
he was cross and grouchy.

One night during that important Advent Wali Ali was leading
us in a dance based on the phrase *Ya Azim.* The chant went: *Ya
azim, hu, hu, Allah hu, Allah hu, Allah hu, Allah hu, hu, hu, hu,
hu, Assalaam aleikhum wa aleikhum assalaam.* Allah, of course,
means God. *Hu* is an intensive; it means God himself, God
present here. *Assalaam aleikhum* means "the peace of God be
with you." This was a "greeting dance": everyone in the three
concentric circles paired with a partner and after each repetition
of the chant moved on to a new partner for the next cycle.

Each cycle began with a bow to the partner on the words "*Ya
Azim.*" From then on, one was turning most of the time. For
what the dervishes and also the Shakers had discovered, and
which we'd all known as children and have perhaps rediscovered
in the discos, is that spinning around can make one ecstatic. As
I was doing that dance, going faster and faster as Wali Ali
encouraged the drummer to speed up the rhythm, I realized the
meaning of the words I was singing: "God himself, God himself."

I moved to the next partner, I bowed, *"Ya Azim."* I saw I was bowing to God. And I realized that not only was the partner God for me, but I was God for my partner. For a moment the world changed. For a moment I saw all things as One—unseparated. The subject-object distinction that is so much a part of my everyday perception disappeared. As I moved on to several more partners I saw that it didn't make any difference whether they were men or women, beautiful or ugly, appealing or repulsive, the dance went on and on.

I remained in that state of vision for the rest of the evening and after I left the hall, I realized that vision extended to everyone, not just fellow dervishes.

That dance was a microcosm of the Great Dance that is God's creation of the universe. The electrons spin in dance around their nuclei, the planets about their suns. The galaxies spin with one another. And they're all chanting: *"Allah hu, Allah hu,* Peace be with you!"

One Saturday afternoon Toby Marotta and I were waiting for a bus at the corner of Castro and 18th, in the heart of San Francisco's best-known gay neighborhood. All around us were men intentionally projecting themselves sexually. It was a warm day for San Francisco and many had taken the excuse to discard unnecessary clothing. Guys wearing only cut-off jeans, some with skimpy T-shirts or tanktops, many bare-chested, were walking or leaning suggestively against lamp posts or buildings. They searched each passerby suggestively, invitingly.

This blatant sexuality upset me. While as a counterculturalist I considered myself liberated, I had very strong notions, many of them learned from the feminists I worked with at the Tenderloin Clinic, about what kinds of behavior were "politically correct." I had notions developed during my experience as a monk about what kinds of behavior were "spiritually pure." And I had notions deriving simply from my own sexual sensibilities. Perhaps because of my political and religious background, I'd come to feel "superior" to people who seemed to me too concerned with their bodies.

Like most such feelings of superiority, I suppose, these were really just compensations for feelings of inadequacy. I've suffered from what might be called the "Woody Allen complex." I've wanted to look like a Robert Redford and to have people desire me for my masculine beauty. But the fact is that I don't look like Redford and do look more like Allen—or like Saint John of the Cross (I could never shake my monkishness). I have been more respected for my intelligence than desired for my beauty. I resented the sexual prowess and obvious good looks of the men walking along Castro Street. These were the homosexuals, I thought, who were supposed to be effete sissies, but here they were, almost all handsome, manly, and vital. Some of them put Robert Redford in the class with Woody and me. Yet for all their good looks, I did not see them as happy.

As I stood on the corner, I watched the men avoiding eye contact as they passed one another. They glanced furtively, looking away quickly when someone appeared to look back at them. They seemed almost afraid of being caught in the act of cruising. I recalled reports I had heard from clients at the Clinic of how they'd felt rejected and put down as they cruised Castro Street. I recalled their stories of the futile hunt for "Mr. Right," the fantasy lover. I recalled their acknowledgment of how such fantasies, based on particular kinds of sexual attractiveness or physical appearance, seemed to keep them imprisoned in only the most superficial assessments of people.

I thought about the myths of karma. I saw these men trapped in webs of their own unwitting design, rejecting and so being rejected because they were looking for a fantasy ideal that just didn't exist, looking for someone attractive and sexy yet missing out because, hoping for some ideal still more attractive and more sexy to come along, they passed up real opportunities.

I recalled my own experiences of walking down Castro Street and feeling invisible, unable to make civil eye contact with other walkers. I recalled the fears that I'd woven for myself a karmic web from which I could never escape. And I thought that the solution—what I often told my clients might bring them some relief—was to cut right through the karma by fleeing from this place.

I was feeling disgusted with all the impersonal sexuality I saw around me, yet struggling to feel compassion for the suffering homosexuals hiding behind their masks of pretended glamour. I remarked to Toby that if we could have some influence in the world, how wonderful and merciful it would be to free these suffering homosexuals from their imprisonment in the sexual ghetto.

Toby looked at me quizzically. "What suffering homosexuals?" he asked.

I described my perceptions of the surging crowd moving up and down Castro under the bright afternoon sun. Toby said he didn't perceive things that way at all. What he saw were liberated gay men, enjoying the sunny day, reveling in their sexuality, delighting in the beauty of their own and others' bodies, showing off to one another, sharing their delight, and exulting in their liberation.

"But what about all the sexual rejection and internalized self-hate?" I objected.

"That's the whole point," Toby replied. "These men are free from fear and self-loathing. They're not suffering queens and oppressed faggots. They're being natural and open in the styles the subculture has developed. They're behaving just like everybody else walking on a public street, acknowledging friends and acquaintances, noticing an attractive face now and then, but being pretty oblivious to the passing stream. Most of them aren't feeling sexual rejection because they're not out hunting sex. They're on their way to the supermarket or the drugstore.

"Of course, most of them are aware of the sexual tension in

the air; they enjoy it; that's partly why they're out here today. Some of them are cruising for sex, especially the ones in the bars," he allowed. "But even then they're doing that because they enjoy the game; it's a sport, a way to spend a lazy afternoon. It's not all that serious to them."

Suddenly I felt in myself an odd change of consciousness. Just as switching the lights from a dim and cold blue to a bright and sunny amber can abruptly change the mood on a stage, so in my mind a filter switched. I saw what Toby was seeing and everything was different. Instead of a repressed demimonde, full of desperate, suffering, compulsively sexual homosexuals, I felt surrounded by gay community, full of natural, happy, liberated gay men. Instead of karma, liberation. I was astonished by how differently I experienced the world around me and how differently I experienced myself standing on that street corner.

"Why do you think they're desperate?" Toby asked, breaking into my astonishment.

I started to explain, but stopped myself, not wanting to spoil my vision. "Well, I don't know; your explanation of it all is much more appealing than mine."

Toby began explaining the liberationist politics to which he attributed the emergence of vital gay neighborhoods like the Castro. I listened half attentively, half noticing that the bus we wanted was coming, and half questioning what my sudden change of consciousness signified.

As we got settled on the bus, I was still feeling dismayed. We both fell silent as the bus motor, revving to carry us up the hill, drowned out our conversation. I was thinking about Toby's question. I saw the men on the street as desperate because that jibed with my own experience and the report of more than one person I'd talked to in and out of the Clinic. I wasn't only projecting my own prejudices or neurotic conflicts onto the scene. But Toby's version wasn't wrong either. Strangely, both perceptions were true. Both realities were present together, superimposed on one another.

"Beauty is in the eye of the beholder. One man's meat is another man's poison," I thought tritely. I recalled the Buddhist saying that the unenlightened live in an unenlightened world, the bodhisattvas live in a bodhisattva world, buddhas live in a buddha world.

The bus crested the hill and started down the other side. The motor groaned as the clutch engaged to slow us down for the steep descent. After a couple of stops it was time to transfer to another bus. I began to explain to Toby, after we'd alighted, how the universe must be very amorphous, never fixed or solid, how it must be that both my clients' reports and his description were equally true.

Toby did acknowledge that there were people in the Castro who were suffering and who did feel the burden of years of homophobic indoctrination and who spread their unhappiness to others. But he wouldn't agree with me that the truth was so arbitrary. He insisted that he could scientifically document his perception. In fact, he said, he was beginning to through his research.

He did allow, however, that metaphysically my point might be valid, and that as a therapist it was logical for me to focus on the experience of those needing help. It became clear to me that my goal in therapy should be to change the clients' perceptions so that what looked to them like a world of misery became instead a world of happiness. Obviously, when people perceive the world as desperate, hostile, unfulfilling, and sick, they tend to act out those qualities and to create around them that kind of world, for themselves and for others.

The conversation continued all through dinner. By the time he left for home, Toby and I had agreed that the way to change things was to see the world with different eyes so that instead of vulgar and threatening it appeared benign and supportive.

FOURTEEN

Seeing Sex Differently

One evening, not long after my vision at the Sufi class, I struck up a conversation with a young hustler. I noticed him because he looked like a flesh and blood version of drawings that had appeared in the California gay press during the early '70s. These drawings of boys with long blond hair, square faces with big innocent eyes, bulging muscles and crotches, and surfer looks were signed "Toby." Occasionally gay men in San Francisco would ask me if I were Toby the artist. This young man looked uncannily like one of the Toby drawings. In fact, I initiated the conversation by asking if he were familiar with them. He wasn't, but he seemed eager to talk and so we sat for a couple of hours and he told me of his life.

His name was Michael, but this Michael was no underworld monster. He was twenty-two now and wasn't hustling anymore. He'd "burnt out" on the street and got a job that paid pretty well. He'd started hustling at sixteen, he explained, because he'd been thrown out of his home when his parents saw he wasn't going to turn out straight and socially acceptable. He'd been devastated by the rejection. He was lonely and lost and angry.

He discovered quickly that his good looks could bring him attention and money. He was happy to be cared for by older men, even if after living with them a few weeks he discovered their lives were so alien he didn't want to stay with them, or they decided they'd had enough of him. But he didn't like being cast back on the street. It made him more angry; it reminded him too much of his parents' rejection. And so sometimes he'd leave the johns, rejecting them first, just to get even for all the rejection he'd felt. He came to understand why the men might lose interest. That was, after all, the nature of sexual attractions and he felt that same fickleness himself.

He'd come to think of himself as a student of human feelings. He saw how unhappy some of the men were who gave him money. He made a point of listening to them talk about their lives. He liked the sex better, he said, when he felt he knew the person a little. And he tried to comfort the men when they needed that. He realized that, just as much as their attention to him had strengthened him when he was first on the street, his attention could help them. The men, especially those who felt old and unattractive, seemed revitalized by it. He was young and pretty and he knew that gave him power to make others feel young and pretty.

He told me that hustling could be desperate exploitation of others or it could be loving service. He'd known what it was like to try to get as much as he could from the johns, demanding more money, or maybe ripping them off when they weren't looking. And he'd discovered what it was like to feel their need and to care for them, if only for a moment. He said the whole experience then had changed for him. He stopped looking for ways to get even with his parents. And pretty soon, in fact, he stopped hustling. He still tricked around and, I think, he still accepted money occasionally, but he had a steady boyfriend and a job now.

Michael seemed to me a little simple, but I was impressed by his motivation. He was a young and beautiful boy. He'd experienced a great deal of pain in his short life. He'd wandered the streets lost. And yet he'd learned to care enough to listen to other people's stories. He wanted to tell me all this, he said, because, once he'd learned I was writing a book, he thought perhaps I could spread his wisdom. He'd seen and experienced suffering in the prostitution trade and he'd discovered that through compassion he could rise above it. Maybe other kids and other johns could learn from his story.

I'd heard similar stories, but as I listened to Michael that evening I began to feel a shiver of recognition. I'd thought *I* had been acting out of the bodhisattva vow when I got involved in the study. I had been pretty sure juvenile prostitution was a wicked and terrible thing and I thought I was being a do-gooder bodhisattva by exposing myself to danger and hardship in order to get social services to save these kids. But here, I saw, was the bodhisattva. *Ya Azim,* I thought to myself in awe. I was dazed by the recognition, and a bit chagrined that I'd missed the message before and had thought myself so heroic in taking this job. The hustlers, the boys hanging out on the streets of America, the girls running from threats of incest and frightened by beatings from pimps—these kids were all bodhisattvas.

Common sense tells everybody that prostitution is evil. The police have to be sent out to stop it. But the prostitution world is dirty, the veteran hustler Sugar Bear had told me, only because society makes it dirty. And now this Michael—bodhisattva— was telling me that if people, the johns, the shopowners, and even the police, and the politicians all tried to see love in it, it would change.

One day on the street not long after that, I saw a young woman whose heavy makeup and gaudy clothes identified her as a hooker. She looked as though she was probably pretty beneath the costume. Walking with her, trying to keep up with her determined pace, was a rather short, dumpy Chinese man wearing a business suit a couple of sizes too small. I stopped and watched them pass, reminding myself that I was being paid to observe such things. Occasionally Toby and I had followed prostitutes and clients at a discreet distance in the interests of observing their patterns. But today I didn't want to follow.

I thought of the girl's young body, her firm and sensual flesh, being pawed by the chubby hands of this lecherous and ugly little man. A feeling of revulsion passed over me. Then suddenly Sugar Bear's message came to mind. I looked again and saw a totally different sight.

There was an older man, a father of a family. Perhaps he worked hard in an office or a shop to earn money for his children. He didn't squander it on things like better fitting suits for himself. His wife, perhaps, was tired in the evenings and, at any rate, their lovemaking had become routine and gradually less and less frequent. Life seemed to be passing him by and sometimes he yearned to hold someone to him, to renew the joy he'd known as a young man, when he was thin and strong and the future seemed open.

And walking with him was a beautiful young woman, a daughter of Aphrodite. She could sense his need and knew she could, for a little while at least, recall his youth for him. She could feel compassion for him and soothe his ache. And maybe she'd spark in him the urge to go home that night and hold his wife and help her to remember how once they loved each other so and to realize how truly they still did. The young prostitute was an angel of mercy, an incarnation of Tara born of the tears of Avalokitesvara, bringing grace and affection to the man's tired body. And in meeting his need, her own needs for money and for affection were also being met.

How different that looked, I thought to myself. Of course, I suspected that the sex that followed soon after I saw them was more like my first impression. But it could have been like my fantasy. It could have . . . if that's what they'd both been expecting. If prostitutes were regarded as angels ("Sisters of Mercy," poet/singer Leonard Cohen called them) instead of whores, everything would change.

Positive and nonsensational treatments of hustling are beginning to appear. *Kevin* by Wallace Hamilton is a remarkably cogent treatment. The novel tells the story of a teenage boy who has grown up in foster homes and is then suddenly reunited with his alcoholic mother, confounded stepfather, and delinquent brother. Kevin's brother introduces him to the street. Into Kevin's life enter many of the stereotypic characters of sensationalistic portrayals, but, as in real life, they are only incidental characters. Most important to Kevin and to most of the real teenagers on the street are the inner emotional conflicts of growing up and seeking love.

Kevin is saved from habitual hustling by a caring gay man who is willing to take a risk and open his heart to the boy. The novel's happy ending seems contrived only insofar as in real life the pressures brought to bear by well-meaning but misinformed lawmakers effectively prevent most such happy endings. Hamilton's characters evade those pressures. Too few people are in reality so successful.

Indeed, in reality the events upon which the novel were based did not end happily. Kevin was not saved. The police returned him to an institution and his would-be rescuer was too fearful of the repercussions to fight for custody. Kevin ended up in prison for street-fighting and public drunkenness. Because society considered the sexual activity so unacceptable, the boy ended up a criminal.

How much everything would change throughout American society if sex were regarded more positively than it now is! As we know, one of the greatest obstacles to such a change is the influence of religion. And yet what could create that positive attitude is placing sex within the religious/spiritual context. This is the function of the mythological images.

Sexual drives seem sometimes out of sync with the rest of our lives. The fantasies and fetishes that we develop can seem so out of character. But for all that polite, church-going society would like it to be so, sex is not all motherhood, babies, and nuclear families arrived at through deliberate and non-impassioned decisions to raise offspring. It can be that, and for some people that may be all it is. But sex can be also a driving hunger that seems unsatisfiable, an involuntary pounding in the blood that suddenly begins in the presence of a certain person, who may not even be available at all, or with the mention of a name from the past or through the sight of a photograph or of the certain contour of flesh of the body of a passerby. Sex can be the urge to be close to someone one loves and respects. And it can be the urge to soothe an itch, to set a flame burning in the heart, or to extinguish one in the loins.

Sex in some ways draws us out of ourselves. In the heat of sexual excitement we sometimes do things we'd never imagine doing in our regular state of consciousness. It draws us beyond our social roles and beyond our carefully constructed identities. It draws us into the realm of the unconscious forces that underlie our daily lives. It takes us into the realm the Greeks called "the underworld," and that the Christians, fearing the archetypal forces, mistook to mean hell.

For the Greeks Hades was the level of consciousness that transcended the personal and individual. It was for them, and is still for us, the world where the gods live and where the myths hold sway with awesome power. In that sense it may be the source of life and meaning for us. But to find it we must abandon ourselves. We do not find it so long as we hold onto our daylight identities. Anonymity is one of the mystical qualities of our sexual experience.

Virtue does not necessarily forbid anonymous contacts and one-night stands. As Toby Marotta pointed out to me rather convincingly, we all value the moments of "anonymous intimacy" that occur with a stranger on an airplane or a train. Sometimes, when all the familiar things that support our identity are missing, we bare our souls and share a delightful moment of deep human contact. We may never see the other person again, though we've made gestures of planning to write, but we've built a memory that will never fade, that will continue to make that day or couple of hours that could have been so bleak so warm and meaningful.

A brief anonymous sexual meeting can be like that. It certainly isn't always, just as conversations with seat mates on a plane aren't always memorable or even enjoyable. But it can be. We can be vulnerable and let the other into our soul.

The new promiscuity allows us to enjoy variety and to cultivate experience. Despite its negative connotations in popular usage, the word promiscuous means "wide ranging," "mixing together" disparate elements. We applaud a person who is a promiscuous reader or has promiscuous tastes in food or music. Such a person tends to be interesting and knowledgeable. He or she can be counted on to bring novelty and variety to a relationship or a conversation. When such a standard is applied to sexual and emotional experience, it can mean, not that one is driven compulsively away from deep relationships or into a string of unsuccessful ones, but that one broadens experience, learns what works and what doesn't, increases one's capacity for giving and receiving pleasure and for entering into relationships with people who through experience one learns to value, honor, and understand.

David Fredrick, one of the men interviewed for *Sons of Harvard* said of himself, "I'm not promiscuous, but I'm easy." In the sexual context, of course, "easy" means easily seduced, like the soubrette in *Oklahoma*, who couldn't say no. But to be easy is also to be lighthearted and open, hopeful and optimistic, free of neurosis. We reassure one another: "Easy," meaning "don't be afraid." We admonish one another: "Take it easy," meaning "don't resist life."

Not all those who enjoy the new promiscuity take it easy. The involvement of drugs and alcohol, especially because of the dependence on bars as locales for meeting partners, and the compulsive chase from one liaison to the next can make sexual promiscuity nothing more than a feature of the fast, destructive life. Sex can be pursued with no sense of responsibility either for one's own life or for the lives and personal feelings of one's partners. Then there is no time to catch one's breath or, in stillness, to pay attention to the demands of the body and the spirit. There is no time to be in love, to feel vulnerable, or to feel comforted.

The problem is the compulsiveness and the insensitivity that limit freedom and constrict the spirit. But these aren't a problem just of sex. Compulsive behavior is unattractive and limiting when it involves work or obsession of any sort, even prayer.

In its truest sense, being liberated means being free from compulsiveness. *Sons of Harvard* (pages 229–230) contains an excellent description of such liberated sexual consciousness in the gay male context:

> . . . this had meant learning how to enjoy recreational sex. The experience of recreating sexually had taught us to see through a lot of conventional assumptions about what was involved in having sex. All of us had learned how to divorce sex from a lot of the romantic mythology that traditional American mores enshrined it in. We had learned how to take it and leave it as sport, how to enjoy it without guilt, conflict, and duplicity. We had become capable of separating it from emotional involvements, personal hassles, and persisting personal, social, and professional responsibilities. This didn't mean that we were incapable of combining sex with love in some of our relationships. It meant that we had learned how to complement our more substantial loving relationships with what some gay men called "varietal sex." Hence it was about unconventional approaches to sex, love, and relationships that we had a lot to teach others by virtue of being liberated . . .

We are not forced to choose between two excluding alternatives: compulsive promiscuity and compulsive monogamy. In a world in which exclusive monogamy is not perceived as one's only virtuous and responsible choice, then a multitude of alternatives appear. And many of them are truly characterized by a commitment to enhancing experience, supporting love, sharing affection, giving joy, and learning to understand and be personal.

That is not to say that there is no place for the impersonal. Indeed, as author and gay subcultural commentator Michael Denneny pointed out to me, by twisting the meaning of the words a little, "personal" comes to suggest the neurotic foibles of egotism that can spoil human contact and "impersonal" to suggest the transcendence of these to some free and open state of selfless interchange. In impersonal, anonymous intimacy there can be contact between people that doesn't rely on the masks and postures they often assume when they are being their regular "persons."

One of the curiously mystical qualities, it seems to me, of "impersonal sex"—in an orgy, in a brothel, or (for homosexual men and, in New York, San Francisco, and Los Angeles, for a few heterosexuals) in the baths—is that one can shed one's identity and operate from almost archetypal, primordial consciousness. And in the sense of "nature mysticism" or of "being one with nature," this certainly is a kind of "nature sex." This was the kind of union with the god that was sought in the sacred prostitution of old, when worshippers came to consort with the priests or temple "virgins," who, because they never entered into sex as themselves as much as in their role as meditation objects and surrogates of the gods, never truly lost their virginity.

But to experience union with the god, release from ego and identity, one must do more than just neglect to introduce oneself by name. One must let down pretenses born of fear and become vulnerable. One must surrender to the primal forces. And one can interpret the experience mythically.

In institutions like the brothels and baths in which such anonymous sex can be found, there may be practical rituals, like leaving one's ID in a lockbox at the door, which one can recognize and invest with symbolic significance. And one can carry that sense of significance into the sexual experience, so that by intention the glamour girl, tired whore, bored little tart, the young stud, or preening piece of beefcake become more than just themselves, become Ganymede or Zeus, Aphrodite or Adonis,

206 In Search of God in the Sexual Underworld

Shakti or Shiva, Radha or Krishna, perhaps even, if one dare, Mary or Jesus. To do this is to become very vulnerable, for it allows the other strange power: it forces one to pay attention to the other, to be compassionate, to recognize the god beneath the surface of individuality.

Stimulants that induce and increase sexual excitement, while seemingly at odds with sex as relationship, can also be seen in another way. Drawings, paintings, photographs, for instance, are capable of easily altering our state of consciousness. Light through a stained-glass window falling on a stone floor feels holy. The representation of a flag waving in the breeze inspires a sense of camaraderie with fellow children of our land. The picture of two persons in obvious sexual excitement stimulates excitement.

Unfortunately, because all pornography is repudiated, we do not develop criteria and tastes for images that can positively stimulate and intensify sexual excitement. Thus we find that what could have been icons and yantras to open and direct energies through the second chakra become instead ugly images of people ravaging one another. Rather than depicting the glories of sex and the delights of love and sensuality, most pornography only shows bodies with bored faces in predictable postures.

During the prostitution study we reviewed pornography. One magazine I came across depicted an orgy of some five or six people. The photos were well done, the book nicely printed, the images certainly arousing and capable of stimulating one's fantasy of being among the participants. But one photograph stood out: as the orgy was progressing, a last person entered the room; everyone present looked up and smiled to the newcomer. The photographer had shown these smiles from the newcomer's perspective. That one photograph somehow changed the entire magazine from being pictures of commonplace sex to a depiction of an admittedly unusual, but not unwholesome relationship between people sharing an intimate part of themselves in their anonymity and in their kindness and delight with one another. Denneny commented that such portrayals of "buddy sex" are positive because they present sexual relationships that appear remarkably free of neurotic (and psychopathic) elements.

The truth is that what people disapprove of in porn is not the photographs, but what they implicitly know the photographs are going to be used for: masturbation fantasies. (Yet for that, the actual content of the photos doesn't matter all that much. Though that is what there are laws about.) Pornography and the whole visually keyed penchant of the male to produce visual fantasies to induce sexual arousal, rather than being objectifying and depersonalizing, can be the occasion for praising the beauty of life as it is manifested in real, sexually attractive and sexually active bodies.

Indeed such solitary sexuality also furthers the intention for a beautiful world: the orgasmic experience reinforces the perception of beauty. It is God who is manifested in the bodies. It is God's beauty that is at the base of sexual attractiveness.

The stimulants to the various states of consciousness (pornography, drugs, or fetishes to sexual consciousness, and icons, incense, or talismans to religious consciousness) connect us with the substratum of mind. They move us with anonymous, implacable power. We can ignore them, surrender responsibility for their quality, fail to profit from them, and perhaps even fall victim to them. Or we can understand them as potent instruments for shaping our consciousness, as crystallizations of mythological images. We can meditate on them, using them to open and close our chakras and direct our energies.

Realizing the virtue in the anonymity of sexual forces, we can responsibly place in our lives such stimulants to the second chakra and the anonymous and often solitary fantasies and pleasures they lead us to. Perhaps acknowledging the anonymity of sex can even help us learn the passages between Hades and daylight consciousness so that we can begin to move easily beyond the surface of the world and discover the richness available there.

Compassion is one of the primary virtues of the spiritual life. The traditions tell us that it brings transcendent vision and it improves our relationships with other people. Compassion is the ability and the willingness to recognize that we are not entirely separate from other beings, that we all share the same life, that we could be in another's situation. Compassion is not pity, or even empathy. It goes a step beyond. It reaches into what is almost a mystical reality.

That reality is usually hidden from us, it is often said, by the fact of our embodiment. We all live within our own bodies. We look out day after day through the same eyes and reach with the same hands for our morning coffee, the strip of tissue hanging from the roll beside the toilet, our own or our Beloved's body, or a child's forehead. We become so familiar with our own perspective we fail to realize that the life that looks out through our eyes and the life that meets our gaze through another pair of eyes is somehow one and the same. The others' experience, because its perspective seems so alien—even when it seems so desirable—is unintelligible and withheld from us. As ourselves, we are never able to be in another body.

But during sex we seem to get so close to another body we can almost imagine what our partner is feeling. We kiss a breast, lick the space behind the earlobe or just beneath the arm, or stroke the inside of the thigh. And we can imagine what that feels like. Giving that pleasure to our partner generates it in ourselves. We can in the contact of organs reach into and engulf the partner so completely that we cannot distinguish the penetration from the engulfing. We can hold one another so tightly and warmly that, especially in the heat of erotic flush, the flesh seems to melt.

Sometimes, when we open our eyes to gaze into the eyes of the partner, we can find ourselves looking back. Suddenly what had perhaps begun as only a pleasurable escapade or a release of emotional tension to ease us into sleep with a familiar body has become, because we were willing to pay attention to the other and feel the Beloved's body as our own reaching out for human touch, not just sex, but vision.

In order to discover that mystical feeling of wonder and insight in the arms of a spouse, the bed of a stranger, the touch of a prostitute brought home because we were lonely and he or she also seemed lonely in the city night, we must have practiced compassion in everything we do. We must have taught ourselves to pay attention to another's need, not just in sex, but in all the activities of our lives. We learn compassion when we pay attention to the people around us: the waiters and waitresses, the salesclerks, the drivers in the cars racing along the freeway beside us.

For, in fact, we are in relationship all the time. We can enhance these relationships, making our lives more full if we simply notice the people around us. We needn't have heart-to-heart talks with all the salesclerks, but we can notice whether they seem tired, despondent, or gleeful, and we can, with only a smile or a touch of the hand, share their experience. We can notice the exhaustion or the determination of the other drivers on the freeway, and we can let them go ahead or slip more easily into our lane. We will feel ourselves more touched, we'll make it home safer, and in the long run—the very long run, I fear—we'll improve the world.

Kindness is one manifestation of compassion. Of course, as Tibetan Buddhist guru Chögyam Trungpa points out, compassion isn't just agreement and sympathy. The expression of compassion can be stern correction, admonition of danger, even punishment (as all parents know). But underlying it is always the sense that the other is not so different from oneself. In the teachings of Jesus it is said: Do to others as you would have them do to you. In the Indian law of karma it is expressed, perhaps more ominously, you will have done to you whatever you do to the others. In bed it can mean that the quality of relationship is improved by sex and the relationship, in turn, improves the sex and opens it out into vistas beyond the body.

It goes without saying that the injection of compassion into sexual activity would radically alter the way the whole society functions. It would certainly change the way the young prostitutes are treated—whether by peers, johns, and pimps, or by social workers, researchers, and police.

Just before the paragraph about the cosmic dance quoted earlier in this book, Thomas Merton wrote:

> The mask that each man wears may well be a disguise not only for that man's inner self but for God, wandering as a pilgrim and exile in His own creation.
>
> And indeed, if Christ became Man, it is because He wanted to be any man and every man. If we believe in the Incarnation of the Son of God, there should be no one on earth in whom we are not prepared to see, in mystery, the presence of Christ. (*New Seeds of Contemplation,* page 296)

Franny Glass had been told by her brother to perform well on the radio show It's a Wise Child for "the Fat Lady." Franny did as Seymour advised, picturing a fat woman, "sitting on this porch all day, swatting flies, with her radio going full-blast from morning til night . . . the heat was terrible, and she probably had cancer." Years later, Franny, grown up and facing the spiritual crisis that was always the theme of Salinger's novels, realized suddenly, breaking out of her soul's dark night, that the Fat Lady had been Christ and, moreover, "There isn't anyone out there who isn't Seymour's Fat Lady."

The world is full of God. We recognize God's features in one another's faces. That is no less true of the hustlers, hookers, and johns. Compassion and understanding, not condemnation and opprobrium, is what they deserve. Even the pimps and murderers. The Michael Holmeses and the Bob Benedicts, they too are embodiments of God perceiving the world. Our attitudes blind us and that blindness dirties the world and leaves us its victims.

Of course, we don't want to end the dance by remembering our divine origins too quickly. But the occasional realization can improve the conditions of the world. We can transform the culture by seeing and living in ways that change consciousness. We can change our attitudes and so change the world. We can create a new heaven and a new earth.

FIFTEEN

A New Heaven
and a New Earth

We may be manifestations of the divine seeking to know itself
and our bodies founts of whirling energy, but sin and suffering
still taint our world. Senseless and grotesque crimes are committed every day. There is pain and suffering on the individual,
corporate, and societal level. And all of this does not just happen
by chance. Actual people commit the crimes. Actual political
and social figures decide that power and profit are more important than peace and virtue. Actual people, though perhaps inadvertently, wish evil on others in order to assure their own success
or righteousness.

The New Right blames the commies and the pinko faggots and
the women's rights advocates for the problems. They decry pluralism and freedom of thought. They encourage book burnings.
Preachers harp on the sinfulness of the country. But nowhere
does anyone cry out for us all to just stop it: to calm down,
forgive one another, accept our differences, live and let live in
peace—before we all destroy one another. No one reminds us
that we're all in this together. No one reminds us we are all One
Being.

Though I urge acceptance of difference, some of those differences, I know, are going to create more suffering and ruined lives
and result in clashes that mean more crime and more hate. The
heart of humankind seems dark. In our deepest selves we feel
broken. We do not do the things we think we should. We let
ourselves get trapped by the Tar-babies and Sticky Hairs. We do
not embrace the cross. We forget our vow.

* * *

Hinduism portrays the gods with both a benign and a horrific aspect. Krishna, the lovely boy savior, appeared to Arjuna as the Devourer of Worlds. Shiva, Lord of the Dance, is also Kali, the Black Mother who eats her children. She is Mother Nature at her most fierce. She wears a garland of human skulls about her neck and delights in suffering and death. Tibetan Buddhism portrays the monstrous side of the Buddha-nature. Its iconography is full of flesh-eating demons. Its lamas blow trumpets made of human thigh bones and drink from cups made of skulls. In the initiation ritual called Chod the meditator must spend the night in a grave-yard sitting on a corpse.

The ultimate reality is not all sweetness and light these myths and rituals insist. God is the bringer of hurricanes as much as he is of soft spring rains. For God is not so much the "ruler of the universe" as he is the totality of it. The world that we, with and for God, observe and thereby give reality to is perfect not in the sense of being how we want but in the sense of being full of all possibilities. These possibilities include the cancer and the accidents that kill us and the wickedness of fellow human beings that galls us and makes us curse life.

The world is full of suffering, and deep inside each of us is the urge to murder. The denial of these qualities in God leaves us perplexed with the "problem of evil"; the denial of them in ourselves leaves us unconscious of the seeds that may grow into violence and unprepared for their evil flowering. There are not so much good people and bad people as there are two sides of behavior and two faces of God.

Carl Jung thought that through the shadow, which in each of us is the horrific side of personality denied by ego, was the most direct way to the Self. For to recognize the shadow is to begin to see that one is more than just one's ego. While the lama spends his lonely vigil with the corpse he is encouraged to remember that all the things that frighten and threaten him are but illusions, manifestations of his own thought forms. In truth, he is not the body that will die and rot. He is not his ego. He is the Buddha-nature that observes all these things with equanimity. From the divine perspective there really is no evil because there is no one hurt: God is both the murderer and the victim.*

Facing the shadow in ourselves, or discovering it in others and recognizing its source in our own selves, and then affirming it as part of our whole experience allows us to see the background against which our individual lives are played out. Recognizing the evil allows us to forgive the world and to work with one another to correct the evil, not by imposing our will on others (that does not work) but by understanding their suffering and feeling compassion even for those who hurt us.

The Buddha declared that suffering was the motivation that could drive us to wake up. Perhaps there is sin and suffering in our lives because, as God, we put them there to remind us all one day to wake up from the world-dream. In words that echoed through the '60s with an odd sense of significance, Leonard Cohen said it this way:

> *And Jesus was a sailor*
>   *When he walked upon the water*
> *And he spent a long time watching*
>   *From his lonely wooden tower.*
> *And when he knew for certain*
>   *Only drowning men could see him*
> *He said, "All men will be sailors then*
>   *Until the sea shall free them."*

*Though, of course, Krishna used it to justify Arjuna's ride into battle, this realization in the East is, paradoxically, not taken as a justification for murder and war. For in the long run it implies that the victor is no different from the victim, and nothing can be gained from violence or conquest. It has not been the worshippers of gods with both benign and horrific aspects who have committed war and spread their religion by the sword nearly so frequently as it has

We all live tossed by the sea. We do not know where we'll be tomorrow or when the sea will engulf and drown us. But the sea can free us: it is precisely our insecurity that can release us from the Tar-babies, our mortality that can make us love our lives.

In *Perelandra,* C. S. Lewis devised an allegory of the Fall. The story tells of the efforts of his hero Elwin Ransom to battle with Satan in the person of earth scientist and technocrat Edward Weston for the trust of the Eve on the watery world Perelandra, which earthlings know as Venus. The planet is all ocean; Tor and Tinidril, the Perelandrian Adam and Eve, live on mats of seaweed so thickly clumped that they've become floating islands carried by the sea currents. There is a solid island, called the Fixed Land. There Maleldil, as God is called, has forbidden them to sleep. To do so would be to commit the Perelandrian original sin.

Only after Ransom has successfully protected her from the temptation does Tinidril realize the meaning of the commandment:

How could I wish to live there except because it was Fixed? And why should I desire the Fixed except to make sure—to be able on one day to command where I should be the next and what should happen to me? It was to reject the wave—to draw my hands out of Maleldil's, to say to Him, "Not thus, but thus"—to put in our own power what times should roll towards us . . . as if you gathered fruits together to-day for to-morrow's eating instead of taking what came. That would have been cold love and feeble trust. And out of it how could we ever have climbed back into love and trust again? (*Perelandra,* page 208)

---

been those whose god is all good and all merciful, who hates evil and forbids killing.

That is why we are all sailors. The perils of the sea make us reach out to something beyond ourselves. That perspective beyond ourselves is what we call God. This God is, in Whitehead's words, "the fellow-sufferer who understands." But, as Rabbi Harold Kushner observes, this God is not some omnipotent ruler who answers properly articulated prayers. Rather he is the source of our sense of meaning—meaning even for the suffering. To find Jesus' benign and loving hand reaching out to us, as he reached out to Peter among the waves, or to find Avalokitesvara's, we must place our trust in life.

There are things we all suffer, not because we are deprived or in pain, but simply because we are human and limited. We all occasionally feel the pain of being egos, of being forever unable to escape from selfhood. We all find ourselves acting compulsively in ways we hadn't intended, feeling feelings we hadn't wanted, being possessive, being jealous, feeling petty and stingy, insecure and afraid. Perhaps the greatest suffering of all is that we occasionally glimpse our potential and realize that we are God, free of ego, but cannot seem to hold the realization or the freedom and virtue that attend it. We fall back into the world of time.

In John Gardner's novel, an old priest, teased by Grendel into proclaiming his most prized and personal realizations about life, declares in Whiteheadian anachronism:

> O the ultimate evil in the temporal world is deeper than any specific evil, such as hatred, or suffering, or death! The ultimate evil is that Time is perpetual perishing, and being actual involves elimination. The nature of evil may be epitomized, therefore, in two simple but horrible and holy propositions: "Things fade" and "Alternatives exclude." (*Grendel,* page 115)

Time and space leave us abandoned and alone, forever separated from the beauty we see in a human face, in a sunset, in a mountain valley, trapped in the poignant sense of mortality we see in the yellow leaves of autumn, the death of a friend, or the way our faces change and our beauty withers.

Ultimately the source of suffering is our separation from God. Or better said, the source of all suffering is God's estrangement from himself. For suffering is the price he had to pay for self-knowledge. Had God not manifested himself in creation, there'd have been no suffering, but no knowledge. And that is why the saviors, incarnations in mythic consciousness of God, can embrace the suffering, can go with life and resist nothing.

The suffering, the anguish of the soul observing the pain in the world, observing the pain in its own heart, can gradually burn out the fear and desire that keeps us locked into our own perspective. Dealing with the sexual urges—lusting, rejecting, being rejected, failing, loving, succeeding, stumbling in confusion through the seductive world of the flesh; dealing with death—begging, crying, seeing beyond, struggling to believe, surviving the threats, achieving confidence, regretting nothing—if we bring to these the intention of overcoming fear and desire, can help us exhaust our neuroses and teach us to look beyond ourselves, to rejoice for the others, and "forget ourselves on purpose, cast our awful solemnity to the winds, and join in the general dance."

The saviors' embrace of suffering and the heroes' acceptance of death signify the saving insight: the central Self is so compassionate and so detached from individual perspective that it is willing to give itself up for the others—"Greater love has no one than to give up life for one's friends." In realizing their identity with the central Self, they see beyond death and beyond individual pain. They give themselves up for the sake of the happiness and salvation of all. Innocent though they themselves are, they are willing to suffer for those who are not innocent and who have not merited salvation. That is what we must discover in realizing our identity with the saviors: there is no one for whom we ought not to be willing to die. We must will that all beings be happy.

In the one major account of the Last Judgment attributed to him, Jesus said that the criterion for judgment is not obedience to duty or even to God but rather goodness to fellow human beings. For Jesus, identifying with the Christ-Self, said that as one does to the least of persons, so one does to him. The source of salvation is the recognition of the saviors' identity with all beings, even the least, even the unworthy.

Religious writer Louis Evely cites a story by playwright Jean Anouilh about the Last Judgment. After all the dead are raised and the saved separated from the damned, the saved are clustered at the gate of heaven eager to go in and take their assured places. A rumor spreads through the crowd that God is going to let the damned in too. Everyone's dumbfounded. They gasp and sputter, "After all the trouble I went through! If only I'd known this! Why, it just isn't fair!" Exasperated, they work themselves into a fury and start cursing God. And at that very instant they are all damned. *That* was the Last Judgment.

One of the greatest dangers for the spiritual life is self-righteousness, the feeling that I am better than others. "Woe to you, Pharisees and religious leaders! Hypocrites! You won't let others enter the Kingdom of Heaven. And you won't go in yourselves!" said Jesus. Self-righteousness keeps us, individually and collectively, from recognizing our identity and from willing happiness for all beings. That will for happiness is the only thing that can end the sin of the world. That will is, of course, what is signified by Jesus's sacrifice and why it is said to have taken away the sin of the world.

The antidote to self-righteousness is the will that all beings, whether they deserve it or not, be as happy and as holy as I. This is not an easy thing to will, for it means recognizing their holiness in things my own perspective has led me to believe are unholy. To will the holiness of the hustlers and johns, for instance, or of the Michaels and Bobs who robbed me and threatened my life, is to see that, just as they are, they are as holy and lovable in God's sight as I. That is the saving insight that, on the individual level, frees one from ego and, on the collective, transforms the world.

What will save the world is not avoidance of sin or obedience to laws and regulations, not correct opinions or adherence to orthodoxy. It will not be vegetarianism, meditation, or surrender to a guru, not heterosexuality, monogamy, chastity, or condemnation of pornography. All of these may help certain people at certain times, but they are not absolutes. What will save the world is forgiveness and good will.

The saviors are the symbols of the Self in each of us. Salvation was not what was done by Jesus or Avalokitesvara or any of the multitude of saviors to which human beings have looked but what they showed us we can do. They remind us that we must embrace the suffering of the world as simply a part of our reality. We certainly must not condemn it or justify it as the just deserts for sin.

Jesus declared: "If you forgive anyone's sins, they are forgiven, and if you hold them unforgiven, they are unforgiven." The Roman Church takes that as the institution of the sacrament of absolution and claims that power for her priests. But wasn't that declaration simply that we human beings all have the responsibility and the power to determine what is sin? We can, by our act of forgiveness, continue the Saviors' redeeming acts. Or we can, by our vindictiveness, keep the world unredeemed.

In practice, of course, sinners are those people whose behavior excludes them from society. Sin has most often been used as the justification for excluding certain classes of people from privilege. The sinners were the outcasts. Yet, of old, butchers, undertakers, money-lenders—all of whom incurred uncleanness by their profession—provided services that society could not do without. Today, when sin most often refers to non-traditional forms of sexual behavior, the prostitutes, fornicators, homosexuals, and prodigals fulfill societally mandated functions, especially as entertainers, advertisers, and service personnel. And, to the

extent that they are truthful about their lives, they remain outcasts from polite society. Sexy movie stars may be given a great
deal of attention, but they are, in fact, accorded little genuine
respect or social acceptance.

The kids I met in the Tenderloin, even the bratty and spiteful
ones, were too young, too mistreated, and too innocent really to
commit sin. They were not there because of their sin or their
parents' sin. Like the man born blind who was cured by Jesus in
the Saint John Gospel, their affliction befell them so that the
glory of God might shine forth.

All the suffering makes no sense if we do not see in it that light
shining forth. All the travails of evolution, the life and death of
countless experiments on the part of nature in creating the
human, all are rendered worthless if we do not see in them more
than just random chance, obeying laws of natural selection or the
work of the devil leading us away from God. We must see instead
the gradual growth of intelligence, of God's sense organs in the
world of creation, striving to awaken and recognize its transcendence.

Jesus was not founding a religion of which he was the god. Jesus
ridiculed religion and was finally tortured and executed by the
Inquisition of his day. (How many Christians today, in imitation
of Jesus the heretic, side with sinners and heretics—the prostitutes, homosexuals, low-life wanderers, and fishermen and sailors? Yet, with the exception of Paul, of course, Jesus and the
Apostles were precisely the kind of people religion warns us to
avoid!)

As Jay G. Williams explains in *Yeshua Buddha,* a moving and
convincing book published by the Theosophical Society, the Se-
mite man Yeshua described in the Gospels was revealing the
nature of ego as illusion, and teaching a wisdom for seeing beyond ego. Even (or especially) Jesus' miracles and redeeming
acts are dramatic symbols of life surviving death, of the One Self
rising above ego. Jesus was revealing a truth that any of us can

see when we rise above our limited perspective: we are all one, we are all God. And since all are that Being what else should I feel for myself but love? And that love is most like my own true identity. For that identity is love, the will of being for the universe, the decision to incarnate, the willingness to take upon myself the suffering of the world: God *is* love.

And in the end what will save us is that love. What makes our lives attractive and satisfying is more than anything else the quality of our relationships with one another. Our sexuality is not the cause of the sin of the world. Hate and jealousy and self-righteousness are. Sexuality can, of course, be tainted by those, but it can also be the source and occasion for love and adventure.

Most mythological systems, like those of the ancient Greeks or Hindus, describe the gods performing a wide variety of sexual acts. Occasionally, because of some sexual act, one of the gods incurred the wrath of other gods or of nature itself. Thus taboos were dramatized. But taboos about sex have been only tangentially religious and more directly societal.

The saviors have said little about sexual behavior. The Buddha required that his followers avoid sexual misconduct, which is interpreted as bringing harm to others through one's sexual behavior or allowing sex to dissipate one's meditations and throw one off the path of moderation. The Law Moses brought down from the mountain said nothing about sex but condemned violation of marriage contracts and covetousness of others' belongings (including wives). Jesus said only that a man should not divorce his wife unless she's been adulterous and that if that were a hardship then one should avoid marriage altogether (after all, he said, some men are eunuchs for the sake of the Kingdom). Jesus rejected the practice of stoning adulterers, recognizing that no one is free enough of sin to punish another, for he said, in what was perhaps rhetorical exaggeration, lusting in the heart is as sinful as actually committing the act of adultery. Those were not statements about sexual behavior but about justice, kindness, and

compassion. It is the saviors' followers who have established
sexual rules and regulations. Some of these have been for asceti-
cal purposes, some for purely social control.

The Eastern and some esoteric Western spiritual traditions
have developed elaborate practices for directing sexual energies
toward the awakening of mystical consciousness. Tantric *kundalini* yoga, upon which was based the chakra meditation that
Adolphine Carol taught, for instance, has recommended that
males avoid ejaculation during intercourse—or, in a rather more
demanding practice, after ejaculating draw the semen back up
through the penis—in order to intensify the energy moving
through the chakras. Such practices are designed only for the few
who have the patience and discipline to learn the neural and
muscular control that make them possible. (Despite the spate of
popularity it enjoyed during the mid-60s, prompted by the writings of Alan Watts and pulp novels like *The Harrad Experiment*,
tantric sex is part of a sophisticated system of myth and ritual
and a highly specialized yoga.)

To generalize to the entire population the practices of a few
people who feel the vocation to direct their sexual energies in
specialized or bizarre ways for the sake of achieving a particular
sort of mystical consciousness makes nonsense of the esoteric
teachings. To suggest, as has been done in Western Catholicism,
that because nuns and monks choose sexual abstinence (or some
variation of it) all Catholics ought to suppress sex only dilutes
the meaning of the abstinence.*

*In fact, for far too many religious I have known personally, the observance
of their vows was not to enhance and impel their meditation but simply to avoid
sin in obedience to a Church law they didn't quite understand. Many assumed
that somehow sexual repression would make them more loving people, but that
was hardly the case. Christianity lacks a mythology that could explain how
repression would evoke mystical phenomena. It is no wonder that the sexual
revolution has seen a dramatic drop in vocations to the priesthood and a vast
exodus from the Church of priests and other men and women religious who
have never understood why they were living such sexually unsatisfying lives.

Most of us today do not feel motivated to devote our lives exclusively to the quest for religious experience. We might feel a certain romantic pang when we see a procession of monks moving silently and solemnly through a twilight garden on their way to Vespers. And we might benefit from an occasional retreat to a religious house in the countryside or from regular visits to a nearby Zen Center. But we don't all therefore become monks or nuns. And, while a few of us may be drawn to join that life, even then the motivation to enter religious life is less to see God than to enjoy the simplicity, peace, security, and community that such a life affords. Religious ritual and discipline, meditation, common prayer, chanting, and yoga are satisfying in themselves. And, at any rate, if these activities do not appeal, the desire for mystic vision alone will not hold us in the life. Besides, at least among Christian religious, while prayer certainly provides great consolation, it often never brings full-fledged mystical experience.

But our failure to commit ourselves totally to the quest for vision does not mean we will not experience vision. The failure to renounce sex does not mean we do not have spiritual lives. Though some may choose for a time or for their lives to forego sexual activity, sanctity and mystical experience are not the property of those who have renounced sex. Some of the great mystics led active sexual lives.

Being spiritual does not mean limiting oneself to the activity of the three upper chakras. It means holding all experience within a context—a very expanded and all-inclusive context. It means living on as many levels of reality as possible. For scientifically sophisticated men and women, pursuing spirituality intelligently can mean finding roots of their day-to-day experience that sink deep into the mythical, unconscious, and metaphysical levels of reality.

Most of us would do best not to repress our sexuality but, appropriate to our psychological awareness, bring it up into consciousness, understanding it in the context of our spiritual and mythical image systems. Mythologizing and spiritualizing our sex is much more likely, possible, and workable than repressing and denying it for the sake of God. Our society no longer believes in that kind of god and such devotion only renders our religiousness anachronistic. The task before us is to live our lives the way the modern world shows us and in that to find God loving and indwelling, experiencing and participating in that world.

As Leslie's friend Robin put it, God and sex are the two great issues. We must understand that they are reflexes of one another. They are both about creation and about love. In the past the ways we have understood them have sometimes been so distorted that they have squelched love and created hell. But both can be forgiven and redeemed. For we can find them deep within ourselves when we realize that each of us is one with the creative urge that in the mind orders beauty out of chaos and in the flesh reaches out to embrace that beauty.

We may find that our realization of identity with the divine calls us to leave the world to pursue the mystical experience to the exclusion of all else, that the world loses its savor and that sex no longer seems worth the hassle. On the other hand, we may find that it suddenly gives new significance and excitement to our sexuality. It may cause us to cultivate new virtues in the relationships with those we love.

The realization, for instance, that the young prostitutes in Times Square and the Tenderloin are personifications of the bodhisattva may inspire us to seek to satisfy their needs for stability, understanding, and acceptance. That might mean we'd provide foster placements for them; or it might mean we'd bring them into our homes, risking societal opprobrium to offer intimate and personal relationships into which they can grow.

Though perhaps as one becomes spiritually mature the sexual pressures fade away on their own simply as an effect of learning and experience, being aware of the life of the spirit does not mean putting sex out of mind. The second chakra should not be closed down. The delights of love, the warmth of another's embrace, the pleasures of sexual union, as well as the beauty of a newborn baby and the excitement of watching a child discover the world —all these can add to our virtue.

Despite obvious examples to the contrary on both sides, people who are sexually active and sexually satisfied tend to be more loving and attractive, less neurotic and oppressive to others. It is not obedience to rules that makes for virtue, but consciousness of one's own needs, compassion and understanding of others' needs, and responsibility for oneself. It is not pleasure that is bad, but only the habitual and dependent compulsion to pleasure that excludes such consciousness and compassion.

Obsession with sex is necessarily a dead end. With the inevitable passage of time whatever beauty we possess will fade. If all the meaning we find in our lives is bound up with the flesh, our lives will surely become meaningless. That is one of the reasons that Buddhists meditate on the foulness of the body and that some perform their spiritual practice in graveyards and make chalices of skulls: to impress upon themselves the transitoriness of the flesh. In the grave no one will care how sexy we were.

The body ages, the sexual drive fades. Like flowers we grow past the spring and summer into maturity and death. Like all things organic and biological we rot. Were we products of machines and not of biology we might not die. It is the fact we are sexual that condemns us to die and to make way for our off-spring. If we can understand that all that we have feared and called evil is an intimation of our death and if we can make that departure gracefully, then we need not resent the sex that condemns us to it.

In death each is alone. The relationships that had created our world of experience are cut off and our universes annihilated. We are alone, perhaps, because we are fearful and resentful. Or we are alone because we are going back into God, into the One who is always alone and out of which all experience arose. As we return from whence we came, let us be able to say: "Thank you, I loved life. It was good."

Let us not allow our sexual urges and longings to be sources of pain; let us not allow sex to dominate us or cause us to try to dominate others; let us not allow possessiveness and insecurity to ruin our relationships; let us not allow resentment or disapproval to spoil our perception of others' relationships. But let us rejoice in our bodies and in the beauty they reveal in their flowering; let us wish that joy and that flowering to all those around us; let us enjoy our embodiment so that we have something to take back to God, so that we can assure him that his choice of bodies through which to see the world was good.

EPILOGUE

The Boon

When you learn to love hell, you will be in heaven.

THADDEUS GOLAS
The Lazy Man's Guide to Enlightenment

The study of juvenile prostitution exposed me to a world of sin and suffering. It caused me pain and confusion. It certainly cost me a lot of money. But it changed me for what I believe is the better. As I have come to accept and affirm other people's rights to their own values and standards, I have felt my own life open up. I have come to feel less insecure and less obsessed with my own sexuality. My self-image has improved. I feel less driven. I understand my sexual feelings, in all their variety, as integral to my spiritual life.

I've always been rather self-abnegating and self-effacing, though that was not so much a virtue, I suspect, as a neurotic trait. It was always with a certain resentfulness and zealous self-righteousness that I did the acts of self-denial I'd been taught through years of religious conditioning. Now the resentment and righteousness seem to be gone. I no longer think of myself as self-abnegating or self-effacing. I see that my patterns of behavior have not changed much, but now I find I am contented more with whatever comes my way. Calling it self-denial only seems melodramatic. I trust life, simplicity seems to me a treasure and a delight, and best of all, I feel more loving and more loved.

I see that the reason for this episode in my life has been to reveal in me Jesus the hero who came to dwell among sinners. I learned I could also love the sinners. I could understand their lives and motives. I learned I could see the hero in them as I tried to see it in myself. Thus I earned the right to see the Tenderloin in a less negative light than most other people. I earned the right to see my world redeemed and myself resurrected. I earned my right to be a hero. I completed the mythic cycle. My life had become meaningful.

Suffering is the weight that keeps us grounded. It is what keeps God from waking up too quickly and recognizing who he, and we, all really are. It is also the goad and reminder that we can and should wake up. It forces us to reach out, to change our lives, to keep the perspectives always changing. We are all sailors drowning in the sea, hapless victims thrashing about in fear. What every drowning victim must remember is that when you stop thrashing about, you can float. But to do so, you must overcome your fear and stop resisting. That was my spiritual discovery in the sexual underworld.

That was also the political and social service discovery. There is pain and suffering in the underworld. Prostitution does irreparable damage to some lives. No one should have to sell sex in order to survive. But prostitution can't be isolated from all the other problems in society. For some people the alternatives are worse than prostitution. What people imagine about prostitution is far worse than it really is. We can't stop prostitution by resisting it. Given the realities of our world we must accept it and understand it as the chosen life-style of some people whose rights are just as sacred as ours and who are, just as much as we, eyes of God in the world. Only then can we begin to change it, or better said, to watch it change. We can see the best of all possible worlds grow up where we least expected when we begin to allow that the best of all possible worlds doesn't look like what I—or you—think, but what a vast multitude of us, with many different opinions all create together when we wish the best for one another.

It may seem naive to say that in the end all we really need is love, and that love alone is capable of solving social problems. But that is the advice of higher authorities than I. Almost all the spiritual and philosophical teachers of East and West have agreed in the end that the saving power is love: love of life and love of one another. Love doesn't mean feeling maudlin sentimentality and it doesn't mean being free from pain and conflict. Love means finding the wonder in those we love. It means recognizing our mutuality and the common intention, however peculiarly inflected by its particular perspective, of the radical Self in each of us to be happy. In that sense, love means "raising our consciousness" and changing our attitudes.

We need police and we need social services; we need government and institutions. But the proliferation of programs and institutions won't solve our problems. These will not work unless we change our attitudes. Not law enforcement, family reunification, or social service provision, but only a change in the way they are perceived by society at large and treated by their customers will really alleviate the plight of the juvenile prostitutes.

In a way I am sorry I cannot end this book by saying that the solution to prostitution is contained in the following five point program. I could then detail the steps. But we don't know enough about the way things really work to design the perfect program: we don't know simple facts about life in the sexual underworld; we don't understand the role of sex in our physiological and psychological functioning; we certainly don't understand the dynamics of nonphysical reality (how prayer sometimes works and where miracles and healings come from); we don't understand the nature of truth. As society becomes more and more complex and we struggle to find institutional solutions, more and more five-point or ten-point or one-hundred-point programs are going to be suggested. And though I'm sure they'll all be wise, they won't work by themselves.

One night I was talking with Harry Edwards. I was about to leave San Francisco, my work on the research completed. I was working on the recommendations to be included in the final reports. I admitted to Harry that, while I thought the practical suggestions I was making good and even insightful, they were still too superficial. It was useful to suggest to social service agencies that they focus on kids in the sex-trade zones, using outreach workers in street work programs, that they hire gay-identified and ex-hooker personnel, that they seek non-government funding, that they cooperate with gay community agencies and cultivate relations with police and city government. "Those suggestions might help some individuals, but they really won't affect the social problem," I said, with a tone of resignation in my voice.

"Of course not," responded my Wise Old Man. "The problem isn't a problem with the system. You can't solve it by changing the system. Prostitution is a problem of consciousness."

I asked him to explain that.

"Well, people's basic attitudes toward life are what manifest as their reality. We're all worried about the future; we're all scared; we're all on the edge of survival. We believe in a world that is totally hung up on money. And most of us have stopped believing anything else matters. So what we see in the world is a lot of prostitution, because prostitution is equating basic human emotions like sex and love with money."

Harry had been a major source of information for me about life in the underworld. It was he who had pointed out to me in the first place that most of the street kids aren't really prostitutes in the usual sense. It was he who had made me realize that the social patterns of the low-life class are so radically different from those of the middle class that they really can't be explained in terms of middle-class patterns.

"Look, Toby," he said gently but firmly, "what you're calling 'the social problem of prostitution' for the kids is just getting by, making some bucks, and surviving. You may not like it, and it may not be good for them, but you can't ask them to stop surviving."

"But what did you mean when you said it was a problem of consciousness?"

"That in a world in which almost everybody is willing to prostitute themselves—I mean that they'll lie and cheat and they'll work godawful jobs that turn their brains to mush just for money and advancement—you're gonna see prostitution everywhere. Even religion prostitutes itself. All these TV preachers ever do is ask for money; they'll say anything if it'll keep the checks rolling in. If all these people are willing to sell their souls, it's not surprising they see that their children are willing to sell their bodies. Do you think in that kind of a world it's possible to see sex in any other way but as prostitution?"

"So, Harry, what do you do about it?" I asked.

"You have to look at things a different way." He paused, then asked, "Do you know what blessing is?"

I had a feeling that Harry was about to ratify the mystical notions I'd been thinking about in the past months, but been pushing back because they seemed a little crazy.

"To bless something is to make it holy," he went on without giving me time to answer. "But that doesn't change the object. It changes the way you see it. It means you see it in the light of God.

"That's what miracles and healing have always been about. The way to cure disease is to see it was an illusion in the first place and then to put love and holiness into it. I don't suppose you can put this in your report for the feds, but the way to solve prostitution is for all the do-gooders to go down to the Tenderloin and walk around blessing the kids for being there."

"But Harry," I objected, "the Tenderloin is full of evangelists, Jesus freaks, and Moral Majority missionaries already. They stand on the street corners and sing hymns about repentance. The kids just laugh at them. I don't think that does any good for anybody."

"But I don't mean doing that. If those people are going to be down there, they ought to be practicing compassion, not preaching at the kids." They ought to be learning what makes the kids happy and feeling happy with them, wishing them well.

"That's what I meant about blessing. You don't change what you bless, you change the way you see it. It's the religious people who have to change. They're the ones responsible for all the problems. They've got to stop judging and disapproving. God created a beautiful world. God created sex for us to enjoy. It wasn't God that started religion. It was people. And they've used it to ruin God's beautiful world. They started fighting over whose opinion was correct and they turned the world into hell."

Harry's point may have been overstated, but in a way he was right. And in a way the whole purpose of this book has been to expand on that point. We live in "the best of all possible worlds" because this one is the only one that's real, because this one is a projection into three-dimensional space of the greater reality our religions hint at, and because from this one every other world is possible. But when we spend all our time condemning this world and praising some afterlife that nobody knows anything about, we just ruin the life we've got. The mystical teachings have always been about how to discover the Kingdom here and now, how to forgive sin—how to forgive God—and how to bless the world in spite of all the apparent suffering.

The problems that we face in the modern world are, more than anything else, a result of the freedom we have struggled so to attain: freedom from tyranny, freedom from ignorance, freedom from mere convention. That freedom means there is a greater range of possibility in our lives. And whenever there is greater possibility there will be some who choose even the ugliest alternative. But, in the long run, the freedom is more important than the individuals who make bad choices or are forced into unfortunate situations. For without the freedom we cannot fully love our lives.

All of us approach the world from a specific history, a specific place in time and space, a specific set of experiences. We are who we are. We each have a station. The goal of the religious life must be less to change our station to that of someone else (in order to live in that reality) than to work to sanctify and save the reality we perceive as our own. We do this by loving our own experience and by willing that all others love theirs. Thus we must not impose our reality on the others, but respect the rights of each to live the reality of his or her own choice. In fact, we must love their realities, or at least love that they have their own realities separate from ours. Judging another's life vulgar or stupid only makes our own life seem vulgar and stupid, for we must live in the world we create by our judgments.

The station from which some people will experience the world may seem to us terrible, sinful, immoral. But if, rather than hating them, we love them for choosing their lives their way, our world will change: we will see it peopled with responsible seekers of life experience, not with sinners. And curiously, I suspect, we will see the content of their searches actually change. The things we now think of as cruel, disrespectable, and disrespectful will gradually disappear.

The solution to the modern narcissism is precisely the pluralism that is the necessary result of radical, enlightened individualism. For the pluralism demands that we respect one another's rights to lead different lives and hold different values and opinions—even about sex.

The sexual revolution isn't going to go away, teenagers are not going to stop having sex, prostitutes are not going to repent and go home, abortions won't stop, lesbians and gay men are not going to go back in the closet, women are not going to become subservient second-class citizens again, the nuclear family isn't going to be saved, Jesus isn't going to appear and champion the cause of the Moral Majority. But the Moral Majority is right that we have to keep the world from falling apart and we have to do something to alleviate some of the suffering in our world.

This suffering is, more than anything else, a symptom of "future shock." To those with psychological and spiritual insight it is obvious that we have to change our attitudes. We have to adjust to the future. We have to embrace it. And we have to invest it with meaning. My own experience has shown me that the meaning that can save the world is found when we discover God—the central Self, the Hero/Savior, the planetary Mind, the Great Companion and fellow-sufferer—incarnated in our own flesh and heaven manifested here and now.

The truth is that God is not some external personality watching human life from above. Such primitive formulations simply don't make sense. God is intricately tied up with the human experience of consciousness. God is my experience of the greater reality of which my day-to-day perceptions are but an inkling. And I am God's experience of the greater reality—God's own being—as perceived from my particular vantage point. God's opinion of me is my opinion of myself. God's experience of me is my experience of myself. God's love of me is my love of myself. God's love of creation is my love of creation. And God's love of himself is my love of my own experience.

That is why all of existence deserves to be loved just as it is. In fact, it must be loved all the more where it seems unlovable. Jesus said there were two great commandments. The first is that we love God. The second, which he said is just the same, is that we love one another with the love of God. God's love of his creatures is his creatures' love of one another. What saves the world is God's love of the world. And God only loves the world in us, as us, through us. We save the world by loving it.

To love God and to love the world is a commandment precisely because it is not automatic or easy. Often the world does not appear lovable at all. That is when it needs saving. That is when it needs loving. We must remind ourselves that we bear the responsibility for saving the world by loving it no matter how appalled we are at it. (Though, of course, we must also love ourselves for being appalled.)

The best of all possible worlds is not how the world should be according to our opinions and standards, but how it would be if we stopped evaluating it and pushing it to meet those standards. More than the imperatives of moralists trying to get other people to live their way, what will save the world and make it Paradise is our loving and unconditional acceptance of our lives and our conditions just as they are right now, seeing them as manifestations of the divine activity creating and maintaining the universe. For, almost against common sense, if we began to love more and judge less, to be compassionate of others' lives, feeling their feelings, assumptions, views, likes, and dislikes as though they were our own, recognizing the others as reflexes of the same consciousness as we ourselves, gradually becoming detached from and unconcerned about views, values, and the like, beginning to affirm the right of every person to live just the way he or she wants to—if we did this, almost unbelievably, step by step, gradually at first and then faster and faster, we would be reversing the sin and fall of Adam and Eve, we would be transcending the knowledge of good and evil, and we would be restoring to its original visibility the goodness of the Garden.

Our world is beautiful beyond words. Our notions of morality and virtue describe not the conditions we must impose upon other people, but the quality of the world's beauty when we recognize it, when we close our eyes to the notions of good and evil, desirable and fearful, when we break from the Tar-baby and crucify our senses on the cross of space and time and grow eyes that see out of the wounds into Paradise. For behind all the suffering in the world of space and time, all the suffering inherent to incarnation, we are still in Paradise. We bring on all the evil in the world, all the pain in the sexual underworld by our resistance to being embodied. The way to get things to be the way we've always wanted is to take things just the way they are. The way to advance is to stop resisting. When we stop trying to pull it down to us, heaven will fall right on top of our heads.

REFERENCES CITED IN TEXT

Calderone, Mary S. and Johnson, Eric W. *The Family Book About Sexuality.* New York: Harper & Row, 1981.

Campbell, Joseph. *The Hero with a Thousand Faces.* New York: Meridian Books, 1956.

Clarke, Arthur C. *2001: A Space Odyssey.* New York: Signet, 1968.

Coomaraswamy, Ananda K. "A Note on the Stickfast Motif." *Journal of American Folklore,* 57, 1944, pp. 128–131.

Evely, Louis. *That Man is You.* Westminster Maryland: The Newman Press, 1965.

Feild, Reshad. *The Last Barrier.* New York: Harper & Row, 1976.

Franck, Frederick. *The Book of Angelus Silesius.* New York: Vintage, 1976.

Gardner, John. *Grendel.* New York: Ballantine, 1972.

Hamilton, Wallace. *Kevin.* New York: Signet, 1982.

Harris, Joel Chandler. *The Complete Tales of Uncle Remus,* compiled by Richard Chase. Boston: Houghton Mifflin, 1955.

Hite, Shere. *The Hite Report.* New York: Dell, 1981.

————. *The Hite Report on Male Sexuality.* New York: Alfred A. Knopf, 1981.

Johnson, Edwin Clark. *The Myth of the Great Secret: A Search for Spiritual Meaning in the Face of Emptiness.* New York: William Morrow, 1982.

Jung, Carl Gustav. *The Collected Works of Carl Jung.* (Bollingen Series) Princeton, N.J.: Princeton University Press.

Kushner, Harold. *When Bad Things Happen to Good People.* New York: Schocken, 1981.

Lewis, C. S. *Perelandra.* New York: Collier, 1962.

Marotta, Toby. *The Politics of Homosexuality.* Boston: Houghton Mifflin, 1981.

————. *Sons of Harvard.* New York: William Morrow, 1982.

Merton, Thomas. *New Seeds of Contemplation.* New York: New Directions, 1961.

————. *The Seven Storey Mountain.* New York: Harcourt, Brace, and Co., 1948.

Needleman, Jacob. *A Sense of the Cosmos: The Encounter of Modern Science and Ancient Truth.* New York: Doubleday, 1975.

Noonan, John T. *Contraception: A History of Its Treatment by the Catholic Theologians and Canonists.* Cambridge, MA: Belknap Press of Harvard University Press, 1965.

Salinger, J.D. *Franny and Zooey.* Boston: Little, Brown, and Co., 1961.

Sanford, John A. *Evil: The Shadow Side of Reality.* New York: Crossroads, 1981.

Smith, Huston. *Beyond the Post-Modern Mind.* New York: Crossroads, 1982.

Smith, Wilfred Cantwell. *The Meaning and End of Religion.* New York: Mentor, 1964.

Thompson, William Irwin. *The Time Falling Bodies Take to Light.* New York: St. Martin's, 1981.

Whitehead, Alfred North. *Process and Reality.* New York: Harper Torchbooks, 1960.

Williams, Jay G. *Yeshua Buddha.* Wheaton, Ill.: Quest, 1978.